How To Exercise God's Megaton Power Now

Jay Snell

Jay Snell Evangelistic Association
P O Box 59
Livingston, Texas 77351
936-327-3676

How To Exercise God's Power Now Copyright 1994 by Jay Snell. Published by Jay Snell Evangelistic Association, P.O. Box 2626, Pearland, Texas, 77588.

All rights reserved. No part of this publication may be reproduced, stored in a retrieval system or transmitted in any form by any means, electronic, mechanical, photocopy, recording or otherwise, without prior permission of the publisher, except as provided by USA copyright law.

First Printing 1994

Printed in the United States of America

Acknowledgements

I wish to thank Linda and John Weeks for their tireless efforts in transcribing and editing this manuscript. Their suggestions and encouragement were invaluable to me. I also wish to thank the good people of The Believer's Covenant Church who were the original audience of the material contained in this book. And always, my thanks to my wife Corky who endured the long hours of silence as I did the writing on this and the other four volumes on The Abrahamic Covenant.

TABLE OF CONTENTS

How To Exercise God's *Megaton Power* Now

God's Main Source of *Megaton Power* and How You Can Tap Into It Now

Chapter 1: The Dark Mystery Finally Removed From The Baptism in The Holy Ghost Page 7

Chapter 2: Part Two: The Dark Mystery Finally Removed From The Baptism in The Holy Ghost Page 23

Chapter 3: The Bombshell Secret to Megaton Power Revealed at Last Page 37

God's Main Instrument of *Megaton Power* and How You Can Use It Now

Chapter 4: The Linkage of Jesus' Name to The Healing, Prosperity and Well-being God Promised You in The Abrahamic Covenant Page 51

Chapter 5: Proof That Jesus' Name Delivers Everything You Will Ever Need Page 63

God's Five Bedrock Foundations of *Megaton Power* and How You Can Stand on Them Now

Chapter 6: The Two Shocking Accomplishments of The Offering Up of Jesus' Physical Body and What This Does To Power You Up Now Page 79

Chapter 7: The Shedding of Jesus' Blood and What This Does To Power You Up Now Page 91

Chapter 8: The Three Sprinklings of Jesus' Blood and What This Does To Power You Up Now   Page 101

Chapter 9: Your Conscience Sprinkled With Jesus' Blood and What This Does To Power You Up Now   Page 115

Chapter 10: The High Priesthood of Jesus and How It Functions To Power You Up Now   Page 123

How You Can Exercise God's *Megaton Power* Now

Chapter 11: Step by Step Guide to Explosive, Powerhouse Results When You Pray for The Healing, Prosperity and Wellbeing God Promised You and Your Family in The Abrahamic Covenant   Page 131

The Main Source of Megaton Power And How You Can Tap Into It Now

CHAPTER 1

THE DARK MYSTERY FINALLY REMOVED FROM THE BAPTISM IN THE HOLY GHOST

When the people wondered about the man healed at the gate Beautiful, Peter replied, "...why marvel ye at this? Or why look ye so earnestly on us, as though by our own power or holiness we had made this man to walk?"

Two things we must note here. First, the man was not healed by any power that Peter possessed in and of himself. Second, we must note that Peter's own holiness had nothing to do with the man's healing either. What then, was the power and the holiness utilized by Peter to cause this man to be healed. We answer these two questions in this book. And when we answer these two things, we are going to find that the same power and holiness that Peter drew upon are the same power and holiness that are at our disposal just like they were for Peter. In this section we examine God's main source of Megaton Power for both Peter and us. Later, we look at the holiness that Peter drew from. We will see in both cases that they are available to us as well as they were to Peter.

The Baptism in The Holy Ghost is the main source of Megaton Power. The next few chapters contain the most important things I've ever shared about the Baptism in The Holy Ghost. As a matter of fact, this is one of the most important things you'll ever read because I'm going to take some mystery out of what is considered to be a mysterious subject, and I'm going to simplify it for you. A lot of the mystery has to do with the fact that the Greek language, that language in which the New Testament was originally written, just doesn't translate plainly in a lot of areas. It's not a problem with the translation or the translators, it's just that when you take something from one language to another you're going to lose some of it.

In this chapter I am going to deal with two things which are very, very important in bringing full understanding to receiving the baptism of the Holy Spirit. First, I want to bring an understanding of the Greek word "lambano"; and secondly, on the expression "the Greek active voice". I'm praying this teaching will come alive in you as you study intently this chapter. Both of these expressions are vital to your understanding of receiving the Holy Ghost. I'm going to start by showing you the different ways in which this word "lambano" is translated in the Greek New Testament. It's translated more ways than this but they can all be reduced to these four. Let's look first at Matthew 21:33-44:

> 33 Hear another parable: There was a certain householder, which planted a vineyard, and hedged it round about, and digged a winepress in it, and built a tower, and let it out to husbandmen, and went into a far country:
> 34 And when the time of the fruit drew near, he sent his servants to the husbandmen, that they might receive the fruits of it.
> 35 And the husbandmen took his servants, and beat one, and killed another, and stoned another.
> 36 Again, he sent other servants more than the first: and they did unto them likewise.
> 37 But last of all he sent unto them his son, saying, They will reverence my son.
> 38 But when the husbandmen saw the son, they said among themselves, This is the heir; come, let us kill him, and let us seize on his inheritance.

> 39 And they caught him, and cast him out of the vineyard, and slew him.
>
> 40 When the lord therefore of the vineyard cometh, what will he do unto those husbandmen?
>
> 41 They say unto him, He will miserably destroy those wicked men, and will let out his vineyard unto other husbandmen, which shall render him the fruits in their seasons.
>
> 42 Jesus saith unto them, Did ye never read in the scriptures, The stone which the builders rejected, the same is become the head of the corner: this is the Lord's doing, and it is marvelous in our eyes?
>
> 43 Therefore say I unto you, The kingdom of God shall be taken from you, and given to a nation bringing forth the fruits thereof.
>
> 44 And whosoever shall fall on this stone shall be broken: but on whomsoever it shall fall, it will grind him to powder.

This is the parable of the householder where the son and the servants were sent, and they were run out of the vineyard, and killed. In verse 39 the Bible says that when the son was sent, "They caught him and cast him out of the vineyard and slew him." Look at the word "caught" - they caught him. The word "caught" is the translation of the Greek word "lambano". So then the Greek word "lambano" means to *physically grab hold of something or somebody like you'd catch them.*

The "active voice" means that the subject of the sentence does the acting. Here the subject of the sentence is "they" - that is the people that God had placed over His vineyard - and they actively did something. The active voice demonstrates that the subject was the one doing the acting. They caught him. He did not catch them. So the active voice means that the subject did the acting. In this case they caught the son, cast him out of the vineyard and slew him. But they caught him; Greek word "lambano" in the "active voice". Do you see that the word "lambano" in the "active voice" means that those people actually did something? They actually caught the son and killed him.

In Matthew 26 Jesus is giving instructions for the Lord's supper.

> 26 And as they were eating, Jesus took bread, and blessed it, and brake it, and gave it to the disciples, and said, Take, eat; this is my body.
> 27 And he took the cup, and gave thanks, and gave it to them, saying, Drink ye all of it;
> 28 For this is my blood of the new testament, which is shed for many for the remission of sins.

Now look at the expression in verse 26, "Jesus took bread and then he gave it to them and said Take, eat." And then in verse 27, "Then he took the cup". "Take" and "took" is the translation for the Greek word "lambano".. It's also in the active voice. So then, "lambano" means not only to actively catch where the subject of the sentence did something by catching the son and slaying him, but here Jesus is the subject of the sentence and He took the cup, He gave it to them and said, "Now you take it," and then He took the bread - Greek word "lambano". So the word "lambano" means to catch or to take, and in the active voice in each sense it means that the subject of the sentence actually had to do a physical act. Jesus was the subject, and He acted by taking and giving it to them and said, now you act by taking it, and when that was over He acted again by taking back the cup. So we find that the Greek word "lambano" means to take and to catch. And we find in the "active voice" that it's the subject of the sentence that is actually doing something.

So here we find in the first two instances that there was a deliberate act of the will that went in to a physical activity. Before Jesus took the bread and the cup, there had to be an act of His will to do so, and then He followed with a physical activity. Before they caught the son there was a deliberate act of the will before that physical activity.

Look at Galatians 2. We are going to see the same word again, still in the active voice.

How To Exercise God's Megaton Power Now

1 Then fourteen years after I went up again to Jerusalem with Barnabas, and took Titus with me also.

2 And I went up by revelation, and communicated unto them that gospel which I preach among the Gentiles, but privately to them which were of reputation, lest by any means I should run, or had run, in vain.

3 But neither Titus, who was with me, being a Greek, was compelled to be circumcised:

4 And that because of false brethren unawares brought in, who came in privily to spy out our liberty which we have in Christ Jesus, that they might bring us into bondage:

5 To whom we gave place by subjection, no, not for an hour; that the truth of the gospel might continue with you.

6 But of these who seemed to be somewhat, (whatsoever they were, it maketh no matter to me: God accepteth no man's person:) for they who seemed to be somewhat in conference added nothing to me:

7 But contrariwise, when they saw that the gospel of the uncircumcision was committed unto me, as the gospel of the circumcision was unto Peter;

8 (For he that wrought effectually in Peter to the apostleship of the circumcision, the same was mighty in me toward the Gentiles:)

9 And when James, Cephas, and John, who seemed to be pillars, perceived the grace that was given unto me, they gave to me and Barnabas the right hands of fellowship; that we should go unto the heathen, and they unto the circumcision.

Here Paul is talking to the church at Galatia about a bunch of stuffed shirts, a bunch of pseudo-intellectuals who were presenting themselves to know more than Paul about the things of Christ, and Paul is sort of writing to ruffle their feathers a little bit and put them back in their place. He said in verse 6, "But of these who seem to be somewhat...", whatever they were - in other words, they went around seeming to be more than they were - "it maketh no matter to me. God accepteth no man's person: for they who seemed to be somewhat in conference added nothing to me."

Look at the word accepteth. God accepteth no man's person. Here the word accepteth is the same translation of the Greek word "lambano". In this phrase God is the subject and it's in the active voice. So it says, God accepts - or in this case it's in the negative - God does not accept any man's person. In other words, if you're a big shot or the littlest guy in the church, it doesn't matter. God won't accept you because you're a big shot.

God does not "lambano" anybody's person based on whether or not they're a big shot. In other words, "accept" means to accept with your mind, with your heart, with your spirit. It's the same in the mental realm that taking is in the physical. "Accept" is the Greek word "lambano". I take something, I catch something, I accept something. It all means the same thing. That's the third case of the word "lambano".

I want you to notice something in all three cases. It's in the active voice, which means that the subject acted. Jesus acted by taking the cup and the bread. Those people in the vineyard acted by taking the son and killing him. In the last verse God acted by accepting negatively no man's person.

But they did something. The subject always did something. Active means the subject in the sentence did something. Now let me show you something else in Matthew 13.

> Matt 13:18-23
> 18 Hear ye therefore the parable of the sower.
> 19 When any one heareth the word of the kingdom, and understandeth it not, then cometh the wicked one, and catcheth away that which was sown in his heart. This is he which received seed by the way side.

> 20 But he that received the seed into stony places, the same is he that heareth the word, and anon with joy receiveth it;
> 21 Yet hath he not root in himself, but dureth for a while: for when tribulation or persecution ariseth because of the word, by and by he is offended.
> 22 He also that received seed among the thorns is he that heareth the word; and the care of this world, and the deceitfulness of riches, choke the word, and he becometh unfruitful.
> 23 But he that received seed into the good ground is he that heareth the word, and understandeth it; which also beareth fruit, and bringeth forth, some an hundredfold, some sixty, some thirty.

This is the parable of the sower. Various kinds of seeds are planted on various kinds of ground. Now in verse 20 we have the same word translated in a way that is most deceptive. It says, "He that received the seed in stony ground places, the same is he that heareth the word and immediately with joy receiveth it." Do you see the words "receiveth it"? This is a different Greek word from the one translated "received" at the beginning of the verse. It's the same English word but two different Greek words.

The one we're interested in is the last one. It talks about the one that has the seed sown on the stony ground and with joy receives it. That word is the same Greek word "lambano". I want you to notice something that is deadly if you don't know what to look for. The word "receive" is a word that has a built in feeling about it that puts it, not in the active voice, but in the passive. For it looks as though you get it without doing anything. You're just sitting there and suddenly God will zap you. I had seed planted in me so I just sit there and take it. But that is not the case at all. It's the same Greek word "lambano" in the active voice.

So what it really means is, that the person who had the seed sown on the stony ground has to actively take the seed that was sown. That's the full meaning of this scripture. He actually accepted the seed that was sown. He actually did something. He actually received the seed. He actually caught the seed. He actually took the seed. He actually reached out and grabbed hold of the seed. The same word that's translated receive in the active voice means to literally reach out, grab hold on it, and take it!

Now you see how that it looks like "receive" is passive, where I just sit there and do nothing and let God zap me with seed? Do you see how that looks? That's not at all what it means. Not when you take it apart from the Greek. Brother Jay, where are you headed with this? You've shown us four times, four different ways the same word is translated from the Greek New Testament in the active voice. One time they had to catch them, one time Jesus had to take them, another time God had to accept them, now here it is that this person has to actually actively receive the seed.

My point is this. I've shown you two physical actions and two mental actions. But they're both actions on the part of the subject. They're actions. It's not something we sit there and get dumped on us. But it's something we actually have to actively do. Two of them are mental - accept and receive. The other two are catch and take physically. But it all presupposes an act of your will.

Now what I want to do is apply this to the Holy Ghost. Because the same word in the same active sense applies to what you and I as Christians do with the Holy Ghost. Now, let's get into the heart of this. I want you to look at John 1:12. When we get through with this chapter you are going to have the equipment to overcome some bad misunderstandings about the Holy Ghost, the baptism in the Holy Ghost, and receiving the power from that baptism in the Holy Ghost, because I'm going to unravel this, and we're going to distinguish very clearly between the active and the passive voice not only in Greek but in English. For these two voices, both Greek and English, distinguish the identically same thing. Now I want you to see some things here.

> John 1:10-12
> 10 He was in the world, and the world was made by him, and the world knew him not.
> 11 He came unto his own, and his own

How To Exercise God's Megaton Power Now

received him not.
12 But as many as received him, to them gave the power to become the sons of God, even to them that believe on his name:

Look at the word "received" in verse 12 - to as many as received Jesus. Now here's the same Greek word "lambano". And again, it's in the active voice. When a person receives something in the active voice, they actually do something. Remember, I showed you two physical actions with this word "lambano", and I showed you two mental or emotional or spiritual actions both of which require volition or an act of your will or a deliberate thing on your part. If I accept something or if I receive something in the active voice - "lambano" - it means I actually do something.

If you were standing up here and I was marrying you to the girl you had chosen to be your wife, I would say, "Do you take this woman to be your lawful and wedded wife before God?" And you would say, "I do, brother." That's the Greek word "lambano" in the active sense. You are taking somebody, you are receiving somebody, you are accepting somebody, but you are the one that's doing it. You're not just sitting there getting passively zapped. You do it!

Everybody here knows the meaning of John 1:12 - as many as received Him. The question is, "Have you received Christ as your personal Savior." Everybody that names the name of Jesus knows the meaning of the Greek word "lambano" in the active voice when I put it in that context. "Yes, I have accepted or received Christ as my personal Savior; therefore, I have been born again." We understand "lambano" in the active voice because that's the word used in John 1:12. If I say, "Have you received Jesus as your personal Savior?", I mean have you actually done something? And that something that you are to actually have done is to have "lambanoed" Jesus Christ as your personal Savior. It's an action on your part! It looks passive, the word "receive" looks passive, but it's not in these verses that I'm showing you. This word is very definitely an action on your part.

Having said that, now look at Acts 19:2. I've shown you these things before, but now we're taking it and nailing it down from the Greek text. We are seeing the difference between the active voice and the passive voice, and I'm showing you here that this business of "receive", in these passages at least, is not passive, it's active. Which means that it's something you do. Now in Acts 19 the Apostle Paul goes to Ephesus, and he finds some disciples there.

> Acts 19:1-7
> 1 And it came to pass, that, while Apollos was at Corinth, Paul having passed through the upper coasts came to Ephesus: and finding certain disciples,
> 2 He said unto them, Have ye received the Holy Ghost since ye believed? And they said unto him, We have not so much as heard whether there be any Holy Ghost.
> 3 And he said unto them, Unto what then were ye baptized? And they said, Unto John's baptism.
> 4 Then said Paul, John verily baptized with the baptism of repentance, saying unto the people, that they should believe on him which should come after him, that is, on Christ Jesus.
> 5 When they heard this, they were baptized in the name of the Lord Jesus.
> 6 And when Paul had laid his hands upon them, the Holy Ghost came on them; and they spake with tongues, and prophesied.
> 7 And all the men were about twelve.

In verse 2, he asks this question, "Have you received the Holy Ghost since you believed?" The very fact that he asks that question logically DEMANDS the phenomenon of a person being able to believe in Jesus Christ and still not receive the Holy Ghost. Now this word "received" in verse 2 is "lambano"; the same word as in John 1:12 - As many as "received" Jesus as their personal Savior, to that bunch God gave the power to become the sons of God even to them that believe on his Name - same word "lambano", same voice - active. Here Paul is saying, "Have you actually actively reached out there and grabbed hold of the Holy Ghost, have you made Him your own, have you received Him, have you accepted Him, have you caught Him, have you taken

How To Exercise God's Megaton Power Now

Him?" This is not something we just sit back and passively get zapped with. This is a great mistake in Christian ranks.

There are two ways to receive the baptism in the Holy Ghost. One, somebody can lay hands on you and you can just be passive and the Holy Ghost can zap you. But there is another way, and I believe this is the predominate way, for it is the way of actively receiving Him. That way is when you, by faith, understand that the Holy Ghost was given on the day of Pentecost, and He's still here, He's never left. You must come to the place of understanding that you can receive by faith the third person of the Godhead, His power and His baptism , just exactly the same as you received by faith the second person of the Godhead, Jesus. Paul was using the Greek word "lambano", and he put it in the active voice.

Sometimes when we pray for people to receive the Holy Ghost we lay hands on them and pray and they get passive. Then all of a sudden they feel something hit them like a ton of bricks and they'll start speaking in tongues right then and there - that is the passive way. That way is valid, it's Bible, it's Scripture, it works. But with some people, God doesn't operate like that. He did not operate with me like that. He dealt with me through faith, and it was not passive at all, but it was something I did. I actually figured out that receiving the Holy Ghost was a different experience from the indwelling of the Spirit that occurred to me when I got saved. It's two different things. When I understood that, I actively took Him. I actively caught the Holy Ghost. I actively accepted Him. I actively received Him. I actively did something.

Now we've seen a radical departure here from the impression of what that little word "receive" in English leaves. It leaves the impression of being a passive thing; you just stand here and wait until the Holy Ghost comes on you and zaps you. That is not at all what it says. This is not something that God does to me by the Holy Ghost. This is something that I do to the Holy Ghost that God has already sent.

What I am doing is unraveling one of the greatest areas of confusion between denominations. Some denominations say that there is no such thing as getting the Holy Ghost after salvation. They are dead wrong. Other denominations, most of whom want to put it in the passive gear so that the Holy Ghost zaps you, are wrong also. That is part, but it is wrong to say that it is all. Otherwise Paul would not have said in the active voice, "Did you actively receive the Holy Ghost after you believed?" If it was just something that you were going to be zapped with it would have been put in the passive voice, and Paul would have said, "Have you been zapped by the Holy Ghost yet?"

All of the translations mean the same thing. If I say that I'm going to take something or catch something or accept something or actively receive something I'm basically saying the same thing. All of it presupposes an action of my will. We have to understand that the receiving of the Holy Ghost is active not passive. It's something you do. God may not choose to zap you.

This is also a reason why many people are never healed. There are eight ways to receive healing in Scripture. One of them requires no faith at all on anybody's part. That's the sovereign move of God where He just zaps a person and they're automatically healed. We see that at Benny Hinn's meetings; people healed all over the great auditoriums because they are in the presence of God. The Holy Spirit fills the place with God's healing and miracle power. That's the sovereign move of God. That takes no faith on anybody's part, God just does it. Sometimes God even heals lost people in these meetings.

But the other seven require faith. They require you to do something. And when you don't do what you're supposed to do, you will never be zapped by the Holy Ghost in healing. A lot of people come to get prayed for and sit back and wait to get zapped. I feel that I have let people down because I haven't taken the time to explain the difference. Consequently some die prematurely because they simply don't know what to do.

It's a fact that God sometimes zaps a person with the Holy Ghost. But it's also a fact that most of the time He does not chose to operate that way. The reception, the receiving, the taking, the catching of the Holy Ghost is something we do. And that is an act of faith. We just haul off and do it. So here's what we do. We recognize that the Holy Ghost is here, He came in this way at Pentecost, He's never left yet, and He's going to stay here.

How To Exercise God's Megaton Power Now

Now I have the choice to either accept Him as the third person of the Godhead or not. If I don't, I don't have his power. But if I do, I have His power and everything He brings with Himself.

The question is, "How do you receive the Holy Ghost?" You talk to Him just like you do to any other person. When you got saved you talked to the Son of God as the second person of the Godhead, and you said, "Dear Jesus, forgive me of my sins and save my soul from hell." You talked to Him, you talked to the second person of the Godhead. You talked, before you got saved, to God the Father as the first person of the Godhead, because you recognized the fact that He was your creator. So you accepted Him, you received Him as your creator and the first person of the Godhead. When you became aware of Jesus you accepted Him, you received Him as the second person of the Godhead, the Savior. You talked to Him, you said, "Dear Jesus, come into my heart, fill my life, forgive me of my sins, and save my soul."

Well, you receive the Holy Ghost the same identical way. You talk to the Spirit of God as a person like you do to God the Father and God the Son. And you address the Holy Ghost as the third person of the Godhead and say, "Dear Holy Ghost, I receive You now into my entire life. I'm asking You to come in and bring Your power and Your blessings and take me over." When you do that the baptism of the Holy Ghost is yours by faith, because you acted on what God said. Jay, will I feel anything? You may, or you may not. Will I speak in tongues at that point? You may, or you may not.

If you don't at that point in time, it does not mean that you can't. You can. You may need some instructions, but you can, right then and there. And sooner or later you will if you're in the right church and they'll instruct you. You may feel something, you may feel nothing.

A lot of times when I start ministering in the Holy Ghost I don't feel one thing. I have learned that I cannot go by feelings. A lot of people want to go by feelings. Brother, the Holy Ghost may make you feel one way this Sunday and another way next Sunday and another way the following Sunday and not anything the Sunday after that. I don't go by feelings because I know I received the Holy Ghost, and when I received the Holy Ghost I know I got His power and everything else that goes with it.

Therefore, I get up and start. And before I'm through things are happening. Sometimes I feel it; sometimes I feel as hot as a firecracker; sometimes I feel like it's on my skin; sometimes I feel it in my mind; sometimes I feel it inside; sometimes I don't feel anything at all, but that doesn't matter. I know the Holy Ghost is there. And if I've invited Him to take over, He has taken over, and things begin to happen in the lives of people sitting out there listening to me. That's the final criteria.

So, I come to the place that I talk to the Holy Ghost. I say, "I receive You, I accept You, I take You now, I TAKE You, Holy Ghost. Come in and get on the throne of my life. You've been in my heart ever since I got saved, but you've been in the foyer. Now I'm receiving you into the rest of my house."

It's an act. It's active voice. It's something you do, and when you do it the Holy Ghost takes over. You may talk in tongues at that point or you may not. If you don't, don't despair, you can. You may not know that you can, but you can. There's always action involved.

The first time it ever happened to me was in the early 1970's. I was a Southern Baptist evangelist preaching a meeting in the Houston area. I got up early one morning and left my home because we were having morning services. I was so tired, I'd been on the road, I was never with my family, my little girls were growing up without their daddy; I could come home and they would barely know who I was. Other men in the church were closer to my girls than me. They were almost afraid of me. You think that won't break your heart? I did more meetings than any Southern Baptist evangelist in history. I did 50 meetings a year; I'm talking about 50 back to back meetings, not just Sundays. I'm talking about 50 solid weeks a year all across the United States. So, I had one in the Houston area, and I was so tired I couldn't see. I needed a touch from God.

As I was driving I began to pray. I had one hand on the wheel and I held the other up; first time I'd ever done that. As I started to pray, all of a sudden I started to speak in tongues. Man, I pulled my hand down and thought what in the world is going on here? My lips tingled like somebody had a wire with a slight electric current running through it and had stuck it on them. They just tingled. I said, "What in the world is this? I'm a Baptist, I don't believe in this mess." I drove a few more miles thinking about it. I said, "I think I'm going try that again." I raised my hand up and out it came again.

You see, you may speak in tongues, and you may not. But you can. A lot of people never will until they have somebody to instruct them and help them and show them what's theirs.

This receiving of the Holy Ghost is an action that you do. YOU receive it. How? Talk to Him. The same way you received Jesus. You accept Him. You came to the knowledge that Jesus was the Son of God, you received Him. You talked to Him. You said, "Jesus, I believe that You're the Savior. Forgive me of my sins, come in, and save me." You did that. And when you talked to Him, He responded as a person.

People, the Holy Ghost is also a person. When you talk to Him, He'll respond as a person. "Holy Ghost, I believe that You're the third person of the Godhead and since Jesus sent You back when He left in order to take up this business where He left off and now You're His representative, I receive you as such, Holy Ghost. Take me over." And that's it.

This is the power that Peter had. And this is the same power that's available to you. But, there's more. Read on.

People Across The Country Are Saying:

The Most Life Changing Thing Ever Written On Healing And Prosperity Are The Author's Four Books On The Abrahamic Covenant:

- **What Are Abraham's Blessings Anyway?**

This Volume Explains Why Jesus *MUST* Heal and Prosper You Now.

- **What've They Done With Abraham's Blessings?**

This Volume Destroys The Modernistic Denial That Healing and Prosperity Belong To Christians Now

- **The Unbroken Force of Abraham's Blessings**

The Main Reason To Deny That Healing and Prosperity Belong To Christians Now, Defined, Examined, Refuted and Destroyed

- **How To Obtain Abraham's Blessings**

A Simple, Step by Step Guide To Obtaining The Healing, Prosperity and Well-being For Every Member of Your Family That God Promised You in The Abrahamic Covenant.

These Four Books Will Build Your Faith To A Fever Pitch. Order Yours Now, Here, Today. You'll Be Glad You Did!

The Main Source of Megaton Power And How You Can Tap Into It Now

Chapter 2

Part 2: The Dark Mystery Finally Removed From The Baptism in The Holy Ghost

John 20:19-22 is a dispensational pivot. There is a lot of argument about what happened in this passage. So many denominations attempt to make this Scripture mean a future event, as if Jesus was saying, "Receive ye the Holy Ghost a few days from now on the Day of Pentecost." But that's not what He said. Read the scripture again.

> John 20:19-22
> 19 Then the same day at evening, being the first day of the week, when the doors were shut where the disciples were assembled for fear of the Jews, came Jesus and stood in the midst, and saith unto them, Peace be unto you.
> 20 And when he had so said, he shewed unto them his hands and his side. Then were the disciples glad, when they saw the Lord.
> 21 Then said Jesus to them again, Peace be unto you: as my Father hath sent me, even so send I you.
> 22 And when he had said this, he breathed on them, and saith unto them, Receive ye the Holy Ghost:

When He said, "Receive ye the Holy Ghost," He meant for them to do it right then and there, he did not mean wait ten days. He did not mean wait until the Day of Pentecost which was a few days away. He meant do it now. How do we know this? Because this passage in the Greek text is written in the Greek imperative mood, and in the Greek imperative, commands never had to do with a future undertaking. As a matter of fact, in the Greek imperative there is no such thing as a future form. There is no way a Greek could give a command in the imperative and give it any form of a future significance. It always meant do it now, especially when that command was given by one who was in authority to one who was his inferior. I don't think anyone would argue with me that Jesus was the one in authority here, and those to whom He was speaking were inferior to Him; and therefore, the Greek imperative meant that they were to receive the Holy Ghost then and there.

Why do I keep saying "the Greek"? Because the New Testament was originally written in the Greek language, the language of the common people during the days in which Jesus lived. So it was a common, ordinary Greek language that they used. The Greek language is a lot different from our language, it's a lot more expressive. As a matter of fact, classical Greek is the most expressive language that has ever been developed. The common Greek of Jesus' day was not quite so expressive, but it was still the most expressive language known at that time and a lot more expressive and exact and precise than our English today.

When a Greek would use a command in the imperative mood he meant do it now, not tomorrow, or ten days from now. So what Jesus said to them when He breathed on them was that they were to receive the Holy Ghost then and there. This is of major significance for this reason. It is at this point that the disciples actually received the indwelling of the Spirit of God. If we used further New Testament terminology we would say that it was at this point that they were born again. Because it was at this point that the Spirit of God came for the first time into their spirits, and they were literally born again.

Somebody might say, "Well, Brother Jay, weren't the disciples Christians? Weren't they saved before this?" They were saved before this, but you have to understand how. Prior to this time there was no such thing as a "Christian", because the Holy Ghost had not yet been given in the way in which He has been in the present Christian era.

How To Exercise God's Megaton Power Now

They were saved because they were born into it, and they were promised that by Abraham's Covenant. And by keeping Moses' law they maintained what God gave them by promise. So they were saved in the Old Testament sense of the word.

Now Jesus' death was the final sacrifice under Moses' law, and when a person received Him as his Savior that was the final sacrifice for his sins under Moses' law. So yes, they were saved both in the New Testament and in the Old Testament manner of looking at it. But here is where Jesus gave for the first time the Holy Ghost as a permanent indwelling on the part of saved people. For in the Old Testament the Spirit of God did not permanently indwell a person, though they were saved. The saved in the Old Testament were as saved as any body in the New Testament; that includes Peter, Paul, or you and I. They were saved.

But in this scripture passage there is a dispensational change in the making. For it's here that Jesus breathed the Holy Ghost. And He, the Holy Ghost, was to be received by these disciples here in John 20, and He was to permanently dwell in them. So when he said, "Receive ye the Holy Ghost," He did it in the form of the imperative which lets us know that He meant for it to happen right then. At this point they became what you and I call Christians. (They were not called Christians in scripture until Antioch some years later.)

Now to argue with this, here is what you have to do. You have to go back 2000 years, dig up every Greek grammar you can find, and rewrite it. Because until and unless you can unravel every Greek grammar that has ever been done in anybody's language and go back and change the language that was spoken, you cannot view this as being a command on the part of Jesus for those people to do something several days away. Therefore, He meant do it then. He breathed it and said do it now. And I firmly believe that they did. Here is where the Christian era, or the dispensation of the church age as we call it, actually began.

Now there is a difference in receiving the Holy Ghost for salvation or the new birth, and receiving the Holy Ghost for power, because some days later something happened to this same group on the Day of Pentecost when they were in the upper room. Look at Acts 2:1-4,

> Acts 2:1-4
> 1 And when the day of Pentecost was fully come, they were all with one accord in one place.
> 2 And suddenly there came a sound from heaven as of a rushing mighty wind, and it filled all the house where they were sitting.
> 3 And there appeared unto them cloven tongues like as of fire, and it sat upon each of them.
> 4 And they were all filled with the Holy Ghost, and began to speak with other tongues, as the Spirit gave them utterance.

There was a space of days between the time when they received the indwelling Spirit at their New Birth, as the dispensation actually changed, and the Day of Pentecost when the Holy Ghost baptized the whole planet. This, according to Peter, was a fulfillment of the prophecy given by the Prophet Joel.

> Joel 2:28-29
> 28 And it shall come to pass afterward, that I will pour out my spirit upon all flesh; and your sons and your daughters shall prophesy, your old men shall dream dreams, your young men shall see visions:
> 29 And also upon the servants and upon the handmaids in those days will I pour out my spirit.

Here it came. God baptized the whole planet at this time. The Holy Ghost came into the upper room, filled it up, sat on the 120 who were there, and then filled them up. Now they had already received the Holy Ghost, but at this point in time He was on them, around them, and in them by way of filling. Before He was just there, but now they're filled with Him. Do you see the difference? In John 20 they received Him by the new birth, but in Acts 2 this is the baptism of the Holy Ghost. These are two distinct acts separated by a matter of days.

Let me say this, what happened on the Day of Pentecost has never been withdrawn. The baptism in the Holy Ghost is still here. Look at 1 Corinthians 12:13,

How To Exercise God's Megaton Power Now

1 Cor 12:13
13   For by one Spirit are we all baptized into one body, whether we be Jews or Gentiles, whether we be bond or free; and have been all made to drink into one Spirit.

Let's learn some things about the baptism in the Holy Ghost. When I saw this, I broke out shouting. This Scripture had plagued me, I didn't understand it, and I have found there are not many who do understand it. But God revealed this to me as I began taking this Scripture apart from the Greek New Testament. One of the greatest problems we have is unlearning some of the wrong doctrines we've had programmed into our minds. I had this problem, and the Spirit of God had a real time with me, but He finally got through to me and showed me what this really means.

The popular denominational view of this passage is this. They define the baptism of the Holy Ghost as the Spirit of God placing you into your particular place into the body of Christ. Well, I can't argue that we are placed into the body of Christ. And I can't argue that this is called a baptism. The body of Christ is pictured in chapters 12 through 14 of 1 Corinthians as a human body, with each member being located in the body of Christ just as each member is in our human body. For instance, my thumb, my little finger, my nose, my hands, and feet are various members in my one body, and they all go together to make up what we call my particular human body. The church is pictured as the human body, with each one of us as members having a different place and a different function in the body of Christ. It is a fact that when we become a Christian, we are baptized or placed into the body of Christ and into our specific place. Some of us are preachers, some of us are deacons, some of us are Sunday School teachers, some of us are praise and worship singers, but all of us do not have the same function. This is called being baptized into the body of Christ. Most denominations call this placing into our respective places in the body of Christ the baptism of The Holy Ghost.

This sounds real good, except there are some real problems with this view which I don't think the denominations can explain. First of all, look at the expression in verse 13, "For by one Spirit...." The word "by" in this Scripture is the Greek preposition "in" - "For in one

Spirit...." It's the same preposition as our English preposition "in". In English I would say, "I am in the studio." You could turn on your television and in English say, "This program is coming right in to my home." This preposition in Greek means the same thing as the English preposition - it means "in". In our English Bible, however, this preposition is sometimes translated by the word "by" or "with", making it function as a word which describes instrumentality. When it functions like that it's called, in Greek grammar, the "instrumental in". But there is no case in the Greek New Testament where an "instrumental in" cannot be translated with our English preposition "in" and still be just as plain.

So what this Scripture is saying is this, "We were all baptized into our place in the body of Christ which is *located in one Spirit, i.e., the same spirit that covered the planet on the day of Pentecost and has been here ever since.*." When we got saved we were all baptized or placed into our position in the body of Christ which is located in one Spirit. For you see on the Day of Pentecost the Spirit of God fell. And Joel's prophecy was at least to that point complete, for he prophesied, "....I will pour out my spirit upon all flesh...." And since the time of Acts 2, out of God's Spirit has been poured some of that Spirit upon all flesh. There is no flesh that the Spirit of God does not at this point rest upon, because of that baptism in Acts 2.

When we receive Jesus Christ as our Savior we receive the indwelling Spirit, but we were already plunged into the heavenly element of the Holy Ghost which covers this entire planet. The body of Christ is located in this heavenly element, the Spirit. What I want you to see is that we, you and I, are located in that one Spirit and baptized into the one body of Christ which is located in that one Spirit as a result of Pentecost in Acts 2.

It might startle you to know that every time the word baptism is connected with the term Spirit or Holy Ghost it is always linked with the word in, and it should always be translated "baptized in the Holy Ghost". How did they translate this passage "baptized by" when the word means "in"? There are two passages of Scripture which talk about being smitten or killed with or by a sword which explains this.

How To Exercise God's Megaton Power Now

Luke 22:49
49 When they which were about him saw what would follow, they said unto him, Lord, shall we smite with a sword?

Rev 13:10
10 ..he that killeth with the sword must be killed with the sword.

The word **by** or **with** is again the Greek preposition **in**. Why didn't they say "smitten **in** the sword"? Here's what they mean by the instrumental in. The Greek would view the smiting and the killing that the sword does as actually being in it. Therefore, you could say that they were smitten in the sphere of the function of that sword, for there is smiting or the capacity to smite and take a person's life located in that sword or in the sphere of the functions that are inherent in a sword.

Look at it this way, you wouldn't take a feather and smite someone because it's not in the sphere covered by the functions of feathers. This is how this Scripture was translated "by" instead of "in". The Greek mind thinks differently and expresses itself differently from the English mind. Their language was geared to enable them to express how they thought. We don't think like they did then. So we have to put ourselves in the place of the Greek and say it like he said it.

So every time baptism of the Holy Ghost, or with the Holy Ghost, or by the Holy Ghost is used, it always means baptism "in" the Holy Ghost. Now if you have been saved you are in the body of Christ - that's automatic - but you are also in the Holy Ghost. This means that the baptism in the Holy Ghost is yours. All you have to do is receive it by faith and start acting on it. For when you act upon it things start happening, because the power inherent in the Holy Ghost begins to manifest itself in your life and ministry. The silliest doctrine around today is the one that some well-meaning folks teach, and it's that you have to tarry to receive the Holy Ghost of God. Let me tell you something. God is not going to pour out the Holy Ghost on the world again. He did it one time. And when He did, the Holy Ghost filled the upper room, covered all the planet, fell on all flesh, and he will not do it again. What we do is accept by faith what He has already done, and when we receive by faith what God has already done the power of that baptism suddenly becomes real to us for we begin to operate in what we already have.

This is no different than the same principal of salvation through Jesus Christ as a finished work. Christ died once for you and I. He came to this earth once and was crucified once for all. He is not coming back again to be crucified for anyone else. It is now up to us to accept His finished work by accepting salvation through Christ. In the same manner we accept, or actively receive, the Baptism of the Holy Ghost. The greatest discovery that I ever made in my life was the fact that almost every thing I ever prayed for as a Christian was already mine. I just didn't know it.

My job now is to build people's faith and show them that they don't have to pray for what they already have. Act on it, and enjoy it. Listen, I am in the Holy Ghost now, right this minute. So are you if you're saved. I am in that baptism that occurred 2000 years ago. I don't have to do one thing to get it except receive it by faith. Stop praying for what is already yours. If you'll do this you'll begin to flow in the power of God.

I've heard people pray the most heart wrenching, sincere prayer asking God for power. Let me tell you something, you don't have to ask God for power. That power came on the Day of Pentecost and it has never left. All God is waiting for is you to start moving in it, because you've got it. If you're saved you are already in the baptism - begin to operate in it. Stop asking God to baptize you, and ask Him to open your eyes so that you can see that all you have to do is receive it.

Your asking God to baptize you in the Holy Spirit would be the same as asking God to send Jesus to the cross to die for you so you could be saved. God did that 2000 years ago, and He's not going to do it again. You receive by faith what He did then, and you're saved now.

Well, God sent the Holy Ghost on the Day of Pentecost, and He's never left. You're in it, you're in it, you're in the heavenly element. He's not going to send Him again, no matter how long you tarry. He's here, He was poured out upon all flesh. Are you flesh? Then He's upon you.

How To Exercise God's Megaton Power Now

You're in the body of Christ located in the one Spirit. So you receive what He did then, and you have power now.

Remember what I previously said concerning the baptism in the Holy Spirit - you DON'T have to tarry to get it. As a matter of fact, it's an insult to God to tell Him you're tarrying when He has already poured His Spirit out on you. I want to again make a distinction between the Holy Ghost at salvation and receiving the Holy Ghost baptism. Read this account in Acts chapter 19 carefully.

> Acts 19:1-7
> 1   And it came to pass, that, while Apollos was at Corinth, Paul having passed through the upper coasts came to Ephesus: and finding certain disciples,
> 2   He said unto them, Have ye received the Holy Ghost since ye believed? And they said unto him, We have not so much as heard whether there be any Holy Ghost.
> 3   And he said unto them, Unto what then were ye baptized? And they said, Unto John's baptism.
> 4   Then said Paul, John verily baptized with the baptism of repentance, saying unto the people, that they should believe on him which should come after him, that is, on Christ Jesus.
> 5   When they heard this, they were baptized in the name of the Lord Jesus.
> 6   And when Paul had laid his hands upon them, the Holy Ghost came on them; and they spake with tongues, and prophesied.
> 7   And all the men were about twelve.

The Holy Ghost at salvation gets you born again and indwells you. The baptism in the Holy Ghost is for power, and there is a radical difference between the two. I know Christians (in fact I used to be one) who don't have enough power to blow the hat off your head in a wind storm. Then I learned about and tapped into the secret of God's power - the baptism in the Holy Ghost of God. When I did the power was there; I didn't have to tarry, I didn't have to wait. All I had to do was operate in it. Denominational teaching does all kinds of things to try and explain this away. They say that the expression "have you received the Holy Ghost since you believed" means did you receive the Holy Ghost *when* you believed, taking it from the past into the present and making receive The Holy Ghost occur the same time as believing. But this is not what the Greek text says, and it's not what common sense says either.

The expression "did you receive the Holy Ghost since you believed" is structured in the form of a certain kind of participle in the Greek text, and this participle means this - it has to do with a finished action that occurs prior to the time of the main verb in the sentence. The main verb in this sentence is "received"; therefore, the participle makes this statement to mean "having previously believed, have ye received The Holy Ghost?" In other words, did you receive in the past - finished act, received in the past - the Holy Ghost prior to the time of your believing. So people are on shaky ground when they say that this should be translated "did you received the Holy Ghost simultaneous with believing", because that's not what it says.

Let's assume for a moment this denominational belief is right. Let's assume that they have the Greek language down to a science (which they don't) - but let's assume they do. And let's assume that the participle was really supposed to be translated "did you receive the Holy Ghost simultaneous with believing in Christ as your Savior." Let me give you a logical argument against this. The fact that Paul framed the question implies that it's possible to receive Christ as your Savior and not receive the Holy Ghost in the manner in which he is speaking of here. Otherwise, why would he ask a question like this? The fact that Paul asked this question implies that it is possible to be a born again Christian with the indwelling of the Holy Ghost and still not have received the Holy Ghost in the way in which Paul is talking. Again, why would he ask this question? Those people at Ephesus would have looked at him like he was nuts. He just would not logically have done such a thing.

But he did ask; therefore, it is indicative that it is possible, even if these critics are right about their Greek, for these Ephesians to really be saved and have the indwelling Spirit of God and still not have received the Holy Ghost. In Acts 19:5 he told them about Jesus, and they were baptized in the Name of the Lord Jesus. And then when

How To Exercise God's Megaton Power Now

Paul laid his hands on them the Holy Ghost came on them, and they spoke with tongues and prophesied. So it is possible to be saved and still not have received the Holy Ghost in the form of the baptism in the Holy Ghost.

When you get saved, you automatically have the Holy Ghost. Let me illustrate it this way. I performed a wedding once in a beautiful, huge home. When I arrived the butler let me in and closed the front door behind me. He said, "I'll see if they will receive you now." He left me in the foyer (which by the way was bigger than my entire house). Now, do you know who is the most important person at a wedding? It's not the bride. It's not the groom. It's the preacher, because without him or some other officer of the state there is not going to be a wedding. So, I was the most important one there - not me personally, but what I stood for - they needed my name on the license. Without me nothing is going to happen; and this butler said to me, "I'll see if they will receive you". He then turned around, walked away, and left me standing there. And I'm the number one person! Well, in a few minutes the man of the house and his wife came to the foyer and very warmly received me. They showed me through the house, and in fact they gave me Carte Blanche. They said, "Anything you want is yours." They received me.

You can get saved and have the indwelling Spirit of God; and go on about your business and leave Him in the foyer, just barely inside your home. You haven't received the Holy Ghost yet. But when you become aware of the fact that the third person of the Godhead is actually living in you, and He's not a theological concept but is a real person - and not just any person but the third person of the Godhead - you will begin to think, "Good heavens, what have I done to the third person of the Godhead? I have left Him in the foyer while I go on about my business!"

The average Christian doesn't think about the Holy Ghost at all except on Sunday. They don't want anybody, the third person of the Godhead or anybody else, to interfere with their lifestyle. I have found that people love for me to preach hard and be dynamic and evangelistic as long as I don't mess with their lifestyle. But the moment that I do, they resent it. They don't like the Holy Ghost interfering with their lifestyle, and that's the real reason they don't like the doctrine of the baptism in the Holy Ghost. That's the real reason they don't want anybody to tell them that they need to receive the third person of the Godhead, who is in the foyer of their heart, into the balance of their house for they don't want to be bothered with Him. They've left Him standing, waiting in the foyer of their being.

Until you receive The Holy Ghost as a person, you'll never experience the power of this baptism, for the power comes immediately when you receive the Spirit of God as the third person of the Godhead. Get Him out of the foyer and welcome Him into your entire home. When you do, the baptism that came on the Day of Pentecost will suddenly become not only theological concepts and denominational catch-all phrases to explain things away and rob you of your power, but will become electric and will empower you to live a victorious Christian life. You can receive the baptism in the Holy Ghost after you receive Him at salvation.

You don't have a problem receiving God the Father, everybody prays to God. You don't have a problem receiving God the Son. God created, Jesus saved, the Holy Ghost has the power to apply. And all three of them are God.

So Paul said, "Have you received the Holy Ghost since you believed?" They answered, "We haven't even heard of Him." The average Christian does not realize that the Holy Ghost is in them. And they certainly don't realize that He is the third person of the Godhead. To most of them He is an impersonal *It* that resides somewhere in their brain - only when they think about it.

"Well, how do I receive the Holy Ghost?" Look at John 1:12,

> John 1:12
> 12   But as many as received him, to them gave he power to become the sons of God, even to them that believe on his name:

When you receive Him, that is Jesus, you receive Him as your personal Savior. You accept Him at face value. You accept Him in your mind and heart and your whole being as the Son of God. You accept the fact that He died for your sins, that God raised Him from the dead, and He accepted His death as the clean slate for your sins. All this resides in Jesus. So you say, "Dear Jesus, I receive You, I accept You, You are who You said You were, and I want You."

The same thing happens at a wedding. The bride and groom stand before the minister, and he asks the groom, "Do you take this woman to be your lawful and wedded wife before God and everybody present?" He says, "I do," because if he says, "I don't," the wedding is off. But when he says, "I do," he has received her as his wife. The minister says to the woman, "Do you take this man to be your lawful and wedded husband before God and everybody present?" She says, "I do." What she means by that is that she accepts him as a person who is willing to marry her, and she is willing to marry this person. It is an interchange, a personal relationship between two people.

"To as many as received Him....", that is Jesus - a person, the Son of God, the second person of the Godhead as what He is, the Savior - when I say, "I do," to Him, He says, "I do," to me, then I have received Him. When I receive Him, He gives me the power and right to become a Son of God, and I'm saved right on the spot.

Let me clarify something again. When you get saved you've got the Holy Ghost in you. The Bible says in Romans 8:9, "If any man have not the Spirit of Christ he is none of His." The minute you get saved the Spirit of God recreates your spirit, makes it alive toward God, and moves in - but He's in the foyer, because the Holy Ghost is a perfect gentleman. He'll not run over anybody. He'll not come where He is not wanted. He's automatically there at the time of salvation, but He's in the foyer, and He won't move until you invite Him into the rest of your home.

To receive the Holy Ghost you just recognize that the third person of the Godhead is already living inside your heart, and He's been there since you received Jesus. Begin talking to Him, "Dear Spirit of God, I receive you now. Come out of the foyer of my heart and into my home, come into me."

Now listen, there are people going around all over the land telling dear Christians that they can't believe what I'm teaching you. But I want to ask you a question. Are you tired of being powerless? Are you tired of the Devil walking all over you and your family? Then why don't you receive the Holy Ghost just like the people in Ephesus did. Just say, "Dear Holy Ghost, I'm tired of having no power in my life. I've tried to live on my own without Your help. I've listened to Brother So and So, and it's gotten me no where. There's got to be more to being a Christian than what I have. I want to receive You. Spirit of God, please come out of the foyer into the rest of my home and You run my household."

My friend, guess what is going to happen? Denominational blinders are going to fall off your eyes, and power is going to surge into your life probably for the very first time. You will become aware that the Holy Ghost is not a Holy It who sits somewhere between your ears. He is a person who lives within you. He will take over your heart and life, and the power of God Almighty will begin to manifest itself in and through your life and the lives of your family.

Jesus said that God the Father would send the Holy Ghost down here to earth, and the Spirit of God would say and do only those things that God the Father instructed Him to do. And Paul asked, "Have you received that One."

In John 14:15-16 the Holy Ghost is called the Comforter. That is the translation of a Greek word which combines two Greek words; the Greek word Para, which is the preposition from which comes our word parallel (along side), combined with the Greek word Klatos, which means to call. Jesus said the Holy Ghost is going to be called along side. The King James translators viewed that as meaning called along side the believer to be his helper, consequently they translated this by our English word "Comforter".

I believe the Holy Ghost was called along side Jesus to be His right hand man on this planet while He's gone, carrying out what Jesus didn't have time to do while He was here. Yes, the Holy Ghost is our comforter. But the Holy Ghost is the representative of Jesus here on this earth to do exactly what Jesus wants Him to do. This is the One you need to receive. He is Jesus' representative, the third person of the Godhead; not a Holy It, but the Holy One from God Almighty. Have you received the Holy Ghost since you believed? I have, and I can tell you that this experience is real.

The Main Source of Megaton Power And How You Can Tap Into It Now

CHAPTER 3

The Bombshell Secret To Megaton Power Revealed At Last

In this chapter we are going to deal with three key words which will bring a greater level of understanding to Christians in the area of overcoming the enemy and reigning with Christ as the Bible says we are to be doing. Those three words or phrases are "gift", "free gift", and "reign in life". This is what Peter had and it's yours also.

First lets look at Romans 5:15 - 21. I want you to pay close attention to the words "gift" and "free gift".

> Rom 5:15-21
> 15 But not as the offence, so also is the free gift. For if through the offence of one many be dead, much more the grace of God, and the gift by grace, which is by one man, Jesus Christ, hath abounded unto many.
> 16 And not as it was by one that sinned, so is the gift: for the judgment was by one to condemnation, but the free gift is of many offences unto justification.
> 17 For if by one man's offence death

reigned by one; much more they which receive abundance of grace and of the gift of righteousness shall reign in life by one, Jesus Christ.)

18 Therefore as by the offence of one judgment came upon all men to condemnation; even so by the righteousness of one the free gift came upon all men unto justification of life.

19 For as by one man's disobedience many were made sinners, so by the obedience of one shall many be made righteous.

20 Moreover the law entered, that the offence might abound. But where sin abounded, grace did much more abound:

21 That as sin hath reigned unto death, even so might grace reign through righteousness unto eternal life by Jesus Christ our Lord.

Now look at verse 17. It says here, "....they which receive abundance of grace and of the gift of righteousness shall reign in life by one, Jesus Christ.)" Now I want you to seize on the expression "reign in life". A Christian is supposed to be able to reign in life. Underline that expression, put it in parenthesis, draw a circle around it, make big bold brackets around this expression. My question is, if you are saved are you reigning? If you're not, why not?

What do we mean by reign in life? We're supposed to reign as kings. A king reigns. A person who reigns is a person who is in control, he is a person who has the power to do what ever has to be done. The question is, are you reigning today? If not, why not?

I want you to look back at the word "gift". It's used six times in that passage in the King James Version of the Bible, five times in the original Greek, one time in italics which signifies it was not in the original Greek, but it was added for clarification. So six times in your English Bible the word gift is used. What is the gift that is being spoken of here? It's also called a "free gift". What is this free gift? Well, thank God for the fact that verse 17 defines what that free gift is. If you're going to reign in life as a Christian, if you're going to have the power as a king over your own life and circumstances, there are three prerequisites that must be met. Now, it's a given that I'm talking to saved people. If you're not saved, nothing here applies to you. But if you are a saved person you can reign as a king over your circumstances.

Now what are the three prerequisites about reigning in life? First of all, look back at the term "the gift of righteousness" in verse 17. In this passage, every where that the word "gift" is used, it means "the gift of righteousness". Notice also that it is the "free gift" of righteousness.

We need to pause here and define righteousness. In your English Bible the words *just, justified, justification, righteous, or righteousness* are translated from one basic Greek word. This Greek word is a Greek legal term which means "acquittal". So any time you read these words it simply means cleared of all guilt. If you're saved the Bible teaches that you have been cleared of all guilt.

Now put that definition into verse 17. It says, "....they which receive abundance of grace and the gift of the clearance of all their guilt shall reign in life by one Jesus Christ." Do you see this? This thing is a gift. It is not something you earn, it is not something you get, it is not something that somebody owes you, but if you're going to reign you've got to know that you've been cleared of all guilt.

Look at the word "receive". I have already explained this word in the previous chapter. It means to take. The English translation of the word receive is absolutely a misleading translation. It makes it look as though it's passive so that you do nothing but just sit and get zapped. The average Christian wants to just sit and get zapped and "feeeeel" something, and if they don't get zapped and "feeeeel" something they think something's wrong with the church. Look back at the word "receive". That is in the active voice, which means it's something YOU do. That word receive should have been translated accept, not receive. Or it should have been translated take. It's the Greek word "lambano", which literally means to take hold of.

In the parable of the vineyard the owner of the vineyard sent his servants to take the vineyard from those that he had rented it to. Rather than give up control of it, those who had control of it killed the servants that the owner of the vineyard sent. Finally he said, "I'll send my son; they'll reverence him." So he sent his son to get back his vineyard. The Bible says that they caught him and slew him. The word translated "caught" is the same Greek word "lambano" that is used here. They literally had to take the son, hold him down, and kill him. Does that sound passive? It does not. It's something they did.

Now, there is a gift from God to you. God is not going to zap you with it. He's laid it out there and said, "Take it." It's a free gift, and that gift is a clearance of all guilt. When you accept that, then you've got it. If you do not accept it, you don't have it. Notice something, a prerequisite to reigning is receiving, or taking, or catching hold of this free gift which is the clearance of guilt.

Look back at the word receive in verse 17. Not only is it active, but it's in the Greek present tense. Now the Greek present tense has to do with continuously doing something in the present time. So what it actually says is this, not only must you accept the free gift, but continuous action in present times means you have to keep on accepting and keep on keeping on accepting this free gift of the clearance of all your guilt.

Why did he put that in the present tense? Why does that have to be a continuous action? Because somewhere down the road you may want to sin. And at that point if you don't keep on keeping on receiving or accepting or taking the free gift of the clearance of all your guilt, a guilt trip is going to set in on you. And the very moment that the guilt trip sets in, your power stops. Suddenly you are not in control, and when you are not in control you cannot reign in life as a king.

It's vitally important that you understand this. Most charismatic Christians get hung up right here. They think that because they stumble and fall all is lost, and the guilt trip sets in. They want to bolt the doors and head somewhere else where they can get a new feeling that will make them feel right with God. I want to tell you something. People that are always hopping from church to church to church to church hunting a new feeling are about the most shallow of God's little kids! Listen, you may have a feeling and you may not have a feeling. We don't go by feelings, we go by the facts of what the Word of God says.

If you do not keep on keeping on accepting this free gift of righteousness or the free gift of the clearance of all your guilt, Satan's going to back you in a corner on a guilt trip. The minute you get on that guilt trip your power is terminated. You're not reigning, you cannot reign because he's going to say to you, "Look at what you did. Why you can't possibly have any power, look at what you did. You committed this, you did that, you left this off, you did something else." And brother, the guilt trip will derail you. Have you ever been on a guilt trip? I went on 10,000 of them until I learned this truth. And I tell you what, I will NOT get on a guilt trip from the devil over anything. My hope is built on nothing less than Jesus' blood and righteousness. And that's where I rest my case.

You have to accept this free gift and keep on keeping on accepting this free gift. What I did with it last week won't work now. It's when I sin today that I say, "O.K., devil, I'm accepting that gift all over again. How do you like them apples?" And then I'm cleared of all guilt again. If this was not the case then 1 John 1:7 would never have been written, which says:

> I Jn 1:7
> 7 But if we walk in the light, as he is in the light, we have fellowship one with another, and the blood of Jesus Christ his Son cleanseth us from all sin.

How To Exercise God's Megaton Power Now

Every theologian in this world that I know about, even the liberal nonsense theologians, will agree with me that this scripture was written to Christians. That says two things. Number one, Christians have a need for the blood of Jesus Christ to cleanse them from their sins the same as does a lost person. Second, "cleanseth from all sin" is again in the Greek present tense, which means that it's a continuous action. In other words, the blood of Jesus Christ His Son not only cleansed me - past tense - from my sins, but it keeps on keeping on cleansing me - present tense - from my sins. You better master this thing because until you get on top of this one subject there is never going to be any power in you life.

So there are three prerequisites to reigning in power. Number one, accept the free gift. Notice again the word "free". It's a free gift. I want you to notice how much we have. It talks about the abundance of grace and the abundance of the free gift. Abundance means more than enough. God has cleared me of all my guilt "more than enough". I have an abundance of it. And so I begin to reckon on what God says rather than on how guilty I feel because I fumbled the ball.

The difference in me and a whole lot of other people is I am not a goody-goody; I make more mistakes than all of you put together. But I'm still not going to get on the devil's guilt trip! Do you hear me? Because I know and have accepted the free gift of the clearance of all my guilt. This is the number one priority for power in your life. There will never be power until and unless you cross this bridge and settle it. I am cleared of all my guilt, and the blood of His Son, Jesus Christ, keeps on keeping on keeping me cleared of all my guilt. That is the Bible concept of righteousness. Therefore, I am as righteous as God Himself, because I have no guilt in His eyes.

The second prerequisite; you have to receive the baptism in the Holy Ghost. In Acts 19:2 Paul asks a group of people who appear to be believers a question. He asked, "Have you received the Holy Ghost since you believed?" That implies to me that it is possible to be a believer and still not receive the Holy Ghost. Otherwise, why would Paul even ask such a question? Have you received the Holy Ghost since you believed? I explained to you how that when you get saved the Holy Ghost comes into your heart and begins living inside you at that point. But the Holy Ghost does not necessarily have control of your life at that point. It's as if I went into your home and stood in the foyer, but I'm not in the rest of your house. And I can't go into the rest of your house until you let me, until you receive me into the rest of the house. It's only when I go into the rest of the house that I can say that I have an influence over the balance of your house.

Now in Acts 19:2 when Paul asked if they had received the Holy Ghost, here we go again; same word "receive", same active voice. The average person again, thinks that receiving the Baptism in the Holy Ghost is passive. They think that they're supposed to sit out there and tarry and long for and wait and hope, and maybe God will zap them and they'll feel this great big flash and upheaval. They're waiting for God to reach down and slap them in the mouth with the Holy Ghost, knock them sideways, and blind them like He did Paul on the road to Damascus (that was a special case). But when Paul asked them if they had received the Holy Ghost, what he meant was, "Have you accepted the Holy Ghost since you believed."

In many churches the Holy Ghost is not a person, He's a Holy It. He's a thing. He's a force. He's a concept. He's an influence. They don't know what He is, but He's not a Him. He's not a He. He's not a person. But people, the Holy Ghost is the third person of the Godhead. God the Father, God the Son, God the Holy Ghost, and if we can prove anything in this world we can prove divine personality ascribed to the Holy Ghost of God. The Holy Ghost is a person.

Since He is a person what do you do with Him? You talk to Him and say, "Holy Ghost, I receive You, I accept You." That word "receive" in Acts 19:2 should have been translated "accept". For "receive" looks passive, but it's in the active voice which means that it's something you do. Do you want to get baptized with the Holy Ghost?

You do it, God doesn't do it. For in Acts 2 on the day of Pentecost when God sent the Holy Ghost down here, he gave Him one time. And He's still here. He doesn't send Him again for you. When Jesus Christ came to this earth and died, He did it one time. His death is still with us. If you want to appropriate it, you receive it by faith. You accept it by faith. And that one death becomes valid to you for the salvation of your soul.

We use the expression, "God baptized somebody in the Holy Ghost." That's the way we say it, and we know what we mean and so does everybody else. But actually it's as wrong as rain on a picnic to say it like that because God baptized the whole planet in Acts 2 almost 2,000 years ago, and He hasn't done any baptizing since. But what happens is that you accept what He did.

That's what Paul meant when he asked those people if they had accepted or received the Holy Ghost since they believed. It's possible for a Christian to be genuinely born again and go through their entire life believing the Holy Ghost is an "it". That person has never accepted the Holy Ghost as the third person of the Godhead; therefore, they are not walking in the power of the baptism.

For to get the baptism in the Holy Ghost you talk to Him, saying, "Dear Holy Spirit, I receive You now, I accept You now. I know God sent You down here on the day of Pentecost, and You've been here ever since. Now I accept You as the third person of the Godhead. Holy Ghost, take me over, come in, fill me up, come down upon me; for I accept You now. Come in me and on me in power." That's your part. And it's not going to happen until you do that. When you do that the Spirit of God is going to do some things in you and on you.

When you accept Him here's what happens. Number one, He begins to spring up in you like a fountain of living water; for He's already IN you, but now He FILLS you. The second thing He does according to the book of Acts, is come upon you. When a man receives the baptism in the Holy Ghost, the Holy Ghost comes down on him and bubbles in him. He does not come down upon you until you receive Him. But when you do accept Him, He will come down on you, and He will bubble up from within.

Some will ask, "Well, if He came down on me, why didn't I feel anything?" Well, I didn't feel anything either. Thank God I don't go

How To Exercise God's Megaton Power Now

by feelings. There comes a time in your life when you have to go by facts. But some Christians always wants to feel something; and if he doesn't feel something in the feel-good churches, he'll go find himself one where he can. And when that wears off he tears out of there and goes and finds himself another place where he can feel something. I didn't FEEL anything. But I did what I was supposed to do, and the power came into my life.

How do I know it did? Because I can lay hands on the sick, and they'll now recover. That's the power of God manifested that only comes through the baptism in the Holy Ghost. Many times I'll lay hands on people and they'll say, "Brother Jay, your hand was hot as a firecracker", and sometimes I can feel that heat in my hand. Sometimes my hand feels cold as ice, but they're feeling heat. But I just don't go by feelings. What God wants them to feel and what God wants me to feel may be totally different. So I'm content to put the control of the thing in the hand of God and let God make me feel what He wants me to feel and make the person I'm praying for feel what He wants them to feel. But if I don't feel ANYTHING I could care less, because I'm acting in obedience not feeling.

So, do you want to reign in life? Number one, you've got to settle that business of what righteousness is, and do you have it? It's the clearance of all guilt, and yes, bless God, I have it, because the Bible says that God gave it to me as a free gift; and the blood of Jesus Christ His Son keeps on doing the job. And according to the tense of that verb used in Romans 5:17, not only do I receive it today, but I keep on receiving or accepting it from now on - continuous action in present time. For every time the devil throws a guilt trip my way I'm going to throw that word "receive" right back in his face. I going to say, "I have RECEIVED the free gift of righteousness, Mr. Devil. That's means not only do I have the free gift, but I keep on keeping on accepting that free gift, and it's still working. Get out of my face!"

It's a shallow thinking Christian that spends their life running around hung up on a guilt trip. Read the Bible, find out who you are and what you've got. I have a free gift called righteousness. God gave it to me. All I have to do is accept it and keep on accepting it and begin to move out and walk it out in my life.

How To Exercise God's Megaton Power Now

Second, you have to receive the Holy Ghost. You have to take. You have to understand that He was given once, just as Jesus died once. He's not coming back, He's been here. You just accept Him and start walking in it.

There's a third thing we've got to have and that's power. Do you want to be powerful? You've got your choice - you can choose to be powerful or you can choose to feel good. The two are not synonyms. When you begin walking with God, a lot of the time you're not going to feel anything. But what you're doing is being obedient. Do you think Jesus felt euphoric when He went to Calvary? No, he felt pain from seven inch iron spikes. However, notice what He was doing. He was being obedient. And when you grow up enough to stop running around trying to find a feel-good place and find a place that will teach you what to do to obey God, you're not going to need all this euphoria. Now tune me out if you want to and run off like some kid and go find a place where Brother Feel-Good is in there giving you all the soup he's got - where you can "feeeeel" something, but you've still got no power!

Now, do you want to know how to reign? I'm going to show you. Number one, you've got to accept the free gift of the clearance of your guilt and keep on accepting it. Number two, you've got to accept the Holy Ghost as the third person of the Godhead. The average Christian who's never been baptized in the Spirit has never said one word to the Holy Spirit; treats Him like He doesn't even exist. "Well, I pray to God in the Name of Jesus." So what, I do too. But I still talk to the Holy Ghost because He's a person. And He's the one who's living in my heart. So I'm going to say some things to Him. You pull that same philosophy on your wife and you're going to be divorced in less than 30 days. But you treat the Holy Ghost with insult; it's an insult not to speak to somebody who's in your very presence. As a matter of fact, about the greatest insult I know of is to just not talk to someone when they're standing there. For what you're saying is, "You're a nonentity for me; you do not exist." Yet you do the Holy Ghost like that and wonder why things don't happen for you.

How To Exercise God's Megaton Power Now

Look at Acts 1:8 - "But ye shall receive power, after that the Holy Ghost is come upon you...." Jesus is speaking here just before He goes back into heaven and just before the Holy Ghost fell on the day of Pentecost. He said, "You shall receive power, after that the Holy Ghost is come upon you...."

Now, look at the word "receive". That is a key word in the Bible, and I don't believe in all my reading and studying and listening to preaching that I've ever heard that word opened from the Greek text. For it radically changes everything we believe. Again, this is in the active voice. The way it looks in the translation, for "receive" sounds passive, is that I'm supposed to sit like a knot on a log and wait for God to zap me with some power. Well, if He zapped me with power, how would I know that I had it? So if you get zapped with it what good is it going to do you until you know what it is.

But it's not passive, it's in the active voice which says it's something you are going to have to do when the Holy Ghost comes. Now the Holy Ghost came in Acts 2 on the day of Pentecost and has been here ever since. So when the Holy Ghost comes He says, "You shall accept power...."

Put the word accept back in there in place of receive and you've got it. You've got to accept power when the Holy Ghost comes. Well, the Holy Ghost came on the day of Pentecost. So if you have accepted the Holy Ghost, that is the baptism in the Spirit; therefore, accept the power that comes along with it.

A startling discovery that I made in my spiritual life was that I didn't have to get power - I've got it. I don't have to ask God for any thing that I already have. I don't have to sit and tarry and pray to God to give me power when He said that I would have it when the Holy Ghost came upon me. So I said, "O.K., God, I understand what that says in the Greek text. I'm going to act on that. I don't have to pray for power anymore. According to this, I'm going to have it when the Holy Ghost is come. The Holy Ghost came on the day of Pentecost; therefore, power is here.

How To Exercise God's Megaton Power Now

I have accepted the Holy Ghost since I believed. I've accepted the gift of righteousness. I'm not on a guilt trip, I ought to have power; therefore I DO have power." And God said, "That's right!"

So what did I do then? I began to act like I had the power. How did I do that? I got over there in Mark 16 and began to do everything it said I could do. What does it say I can do? I can cast out demons. So I began to cast them out, and little devils began to run. What else did I do? I began to lay hands on the sick and watch them recover.

Why could I do that? Because I have power. I don't have to GET it, I just have to walk it out. Do you want to have power to reign? The key word is "receive". I've quoted you that word in three different verses. You've got to RECEIVE the gift of righteousness, which is the clearance of all your guilt. You've got to RECEIVE the Holy Ghost since you believed - Acts 19:2. And you have to RECEIVE the power that was and is inherent in the Holy Ghost when He came. And He came on the day of Pentecost; therefore,

I don't have to get what I already have. I, according to Jesus Christ, already have the power, for He said, "You shall receive it". So I have to now accept what He's given. When did He give this power? He gave it nearly 2,000 years ago on the day of Pentecost when He sent the Holy Ghost down here. And when He came, He filled the upper room, filled all those people, tongues came, and flames of fire shot all over that room. The place was filled, not only with the presence of the Holy Ghost of God, but it was filled with power; therefore, Jesus said, "Accept it!"

The popular view of this is that I've got to tarry and tarry and wait and wait, and the Bible teaches no such thing. Those people in the upper room had to wait for one reason; the Holy Ghost had not yet been given. Now that He has been given, what am I waiting for? We are not to wait passively to receive, not tarry and wait, but get up and accept what is already yours. I accept that gift of righteousness, I accept the person of the Holy Ghost, and I accept the power He said I'm supposed to accept when the Holy Ghost falls. Since He fell in Acts 2, nobody has to GET power. If you are baptized in the Holy

How To Exercise God's Megaton Power Now

Spirit, you already have it! Now start walking it out, and do exactly what God says you can do in His Word.

Do you understand the concept of "receive"? It's one of the most important words in all the Bible, for it will absolutely change your thinking. Stop trying to get what you already have. If you'll quit trying to get what you already have and start walking out what you already have, I guarantee you it will absolutely change your life. So, what do we do when we receive? We accept, we take, we catch it, we get with it. It's mine; all I have to do is accept it.

When Jesus Christ came into this world he died, and now His death covers the sins of every man who will receive Him as his Savior. It will do you no good until you accept it. For when you accept Christ as your Savior everything I'm saying goes into gear.

But a lot of people that I've witnessed to have said, "I can't accept Christ because I don't feel anything." Nowhere in the Word of God does it talk about what you're supposed to feel like. The average charismatic has overcome this first hurdle (feeling something at salvation), but they haven't been able to overcome the second. They want to feel something at the baptism. "I can't believe the power is operating in my life. I can't believe the Holy Ghost is in my life. I can't believe that I'm cleared of all guilt because I don't feel like it."

Show me the verse where it says you have to feel anything! You've got to receive - active voice - which means **accept**. And when you've accepted you're going to start walking it out. If you'll start listening to me, what I'm saying will change your life. Keep on questioning what I'm saying and go on down to Brother Feel-Good's church and feel good, but your life still isn't changed. For there won't be enough power in your life to blow the hat off your head in a windstorm.

I have a choice every time I preach. "Lord, do I spoon feed this bunch and keep them a bunch of spiritual infants, or do I rattle their cage a little bit and put some backbone in these people so they can stand up and be somebody for God." Even if you get mad at me I'm going for it - that's my choice. I learned a long time ago that if you're going to be in the ministry and do something for God, the first thing you've got to do is quit worring about what somebody thinks about you. You better choose to please God and not man, otherwise you're going to end up on the short end of the stick. The whole congregation can get up and walk out; I'm not changing. God will send me somebody to preach to that's got some backbone and will sit and listen to me preach.

Receive is an active verb which means accept what you already have from the hand of God. It's all free, and it's been laying on the table. Now you can accept it, pick it up, walk it out, and let it make a man or a woman out of you; or you can reject this message and want to feel good all the time, but you'll end up a spiritual pygmy. The day you die you won't be any bigger in the spirit than you are right now.

Do you want to reign in life? You **must** accept the free gift of the clearance of all your guilt, you **must** receive the person of the Holy Ghost, and you **must** receive the power that Jesus Christ said was coming when the Holy Ghost fell and is now here for you.

Peter did. This is the power he had that he said was not his own when the man was healed at the gate Beautiful. This is the same power that is available to you now. Receive The Holy Ghost and you can do what Peter did.

The Main Instrument of Megaton Power And How You Can Use It Now

CHAPTER 4

The Linkage of Jesus' Name To The Healing, Prosperity, and Well-being God Promised You in The Abrahamic Covenant

Healing, prosperity, and well being for your family members is contained in the Abrahamic Covenant. But what is the relationship of the Name of Jesus to the Abrahamic Covenant? Is there a relationship? Is modern theology, even Charasmatic theology, right in just pulling the Name of Jesus out of thin air and going after it? Or is there a specific New Testament passage that links the Name of Jesus to that Abrahamic Covenant? And if there is, what is the significance of that relationship?

Well, there just happens to be one. I'm prepared to say to you that as we move through this teaching you're going to see that you are authorized, as a Christian, to use the Name of Jesus to secure anything and do anything that's contained in that Abrahamic Covenant just like Peter did. For apart from that Covenant, there is no Jesus, there is no salvation, there are no blessings, there is no healing, there is no prosperity; everything centers in that Abrahamic Covenant. Look carefully at Peter's approach in the following scripture:

> Acts 3:1-11
> 1   Now Peter and John went up together into the temple at the hour of prayer, being the ninth hour.

2   And a certain man lame from his mother's womb was carried, whom they laid daily at the gate of the temple which is called Beautiful, to ask alms of them that entered into the temple;

3   Who seeing Peter and John about to go into the temple asked an alms.

4   And Peter, fastening his eyes upon him with John, said, Look on us.

5   And he gave heed unto them, expecting to receive something of them.

6   Then Peter said, Silver and gold have I none; but such as I have give I thee: In **the** name of Jesus Christ of Nazareth rise up and walk.

7   And he took him by the right hand, and lifted him up: and immediately his feet and ancle bones received strength.

8   And he leaping up stood, and walked, and entered with them into the temple, walking, and leaping, and praising God.

9   And all the people saw him walking and praising God:

10   And they knew that it was he which sat for alms at the Beautiful gate of the temple: and they were filled with wonder and amazement at that which had happened unto him.

11   And as the lame man which was healed held Peter and John, all the people ran together unto them in the porch that is called Solomon's, greatly wondering.

We've heard many sermons preached from these Scriptures. As the chapter moves on, the religious leadership gets bent out of shape because this man gets healed. I don't know what it is about religious people that makes them fire-eating mad when somebody gets healed. I've prayed for people in denominational churches and seen miraculous healings take place, but it made the leadership of that church mad. I've had them get up and walk out of the building because somebody got healed; they resented it. I don't understand that. But the balance of this chapter in the Bible is a give-and-take between the religious leaders, because they didn't like it, they absolutely didn't like it. And so verse 12 picks it up, and Peter asks,

> Acts 3:12-17
> 12 And when Peter saw it, he answered unto the people, Ye men of Israel, why marvel ye at this? or why look ye so earnestly on us, as though by our own power or holiness we had made this man to walk?
> **13** The God of Abraham, and of Isaac, and of Jacob, the God of our fathers, hath glorified his Son Jesus; whom ye delivered up, and denied him in the presence of Pilate, when he was determined to let him go.
> 14 But ye denied the Holy One and the Just, and desired a murderer to be granted unto you;
> 15 And killed the Prince of life, whom God hath raised from the dead; whereof we are witnesses.
> 16 And his name through faith in his name hath made this man strong, whom ye see and know: yea, the faith which is by him hath given him this perfect soundness in the presence of you all.
> 17 And now, brethren, I wot that through ignorance ye did it, as did also your rulers.

Notice that verse 13 makes the first reference to Abraham. Now read verse 16. We now have Abraham brought into this thing in the healing of a man using Jesus' Name. And Peter said that God honored His Son, Jesus, and it's the same God who was the God of Abraham, Isaac, and Jacob. Then he goes on to say that in response to this honoring of His Son, Jesus, it was the Name of Jesus that caused that man to be made well. I want to make sure that you begin to see this connection. Now read verses 18 through 26.

How To Exercise God's Megaton Power Now

Acts 3:18-24

18 But those things, which God before had shewed by the mouth of all his prophets, that Christ should suffer, he hath so fulfilled.

19 Repent ye therefore, and be converted, that your sins may be blotted out, when the times of refreshing shall come from the presence of the Lord;

20 And he shall send Jesus Christ, which before was preached unto you:

21 Whom the heaven must receive until the times of restitution of all things, which God hath spoken by the mouth of all his holy prophets since the world began.

22 For Moses truly said unto the fathers, A prophet shall the Lord your God raise up unto you of your brethren, like unto me; him shall ye hear in all things whatsoever he shall say unto you.

23 And it shall come to pass, that every soul, which will not hear that prophet, shall be destroyed from among the people.

24 Yea, and all the prophets from Samuel and those that follow after, as many as have spoken, have likewise foretold of these days.

Verse 19 says that you need to repent. Verse 20 says that He's going to send this same Jesus whose Name caused the man to be healed. He's going to send that Jesus back because He was preached before unto you, and verse 21 says that He's going to be in heaven until the times of restoration of all things which were spoken by the mouth of all his holy prophets. Verse 22 says that even Moses spoke about this Jesus. Verse 23 says that the person that will not hear that prophet Jesus will be destroyed from among the people.

Now look at verse 24; Foretold of what days? The days in which there was a prophet to come that would be the fulfillment of the Scriptures. The day in which through Him, people would be healed. The day in which the God of Abraham would bless through that man and give power to His Name.

But what does that Name have to do with the Abrahamic Covenant? Look at the next two verses.

> Acts 3:25-26
> 25 Ye are the children of the prophets, and of the covenant which God made with our fathers, saying unto Abraham, And in thy seed shall all the kindreds of the earth be blessed.
> 26 Unto you first God, having raised up his Son Jesus, sent him to bless you, in turning away every one of you from his iniquities.

Now, if you will follow the line of those Scriptures you're going to find that Jesus was prophesied about, and Peter finally links Him to that Abrahamic Covenant, because he quotes the last promise that God made to Abraham which is found in Genesis 22:18.

> Gen 22:18
> 18 And in thy seed shall all the nations of the earth be blessed; because thou hast obeyed my voice.

So what Peter is showing here is that the healing of the man at the gate is a direct response to the promise of God to Abraham, and it's the Name of that supreme seed, Jesus, that did it.

Where does this leave us? It leaves us here - healing, prosperity, well being for your family members - it's all contained in that Abrahamic Covenant. Now we find the Name of Jesus being linked to that Abrahamic Covenant, which says to me that I can legitimately use the Name of Jesus to get whatever I need as a Christian, provided what I need is contained in that Abrahamic Covenant.

Now you need to go back and reread this chapter. For you're going to find that the healing of this man through the use of Jesus' Name is directly, according to Peter, based upon and linked with the Abrahamic Covenant. Can you see this? Therefore, God sent that prophet, Jesus, as the ultimate seed of that Abrahamic Covenant, and

How To Exercise God's Megaton Power Now

Jesus gave the use of His Name for us to secure the provisions of that covenant, then whatever I need in that Covenant I can get through Jesus' Name.

Peter was not the only guy that is allowed to use Jesus' Name. Jesus gave us the right and power of attorney to use His Name before He went back to heaven. But since He linked the use to that Abrahamic Covenant means that I can only use the Name of Jesus to secure the things promised me in that Abrahamic Covenant. So, what's promised to me in it? Healing, prosperity, well being for my family, in addition to the salvation of my soul. When I don't have money enough to pay my bills, there is a way that I can get my money; because prosperity is promised to me in that Abrahamic Covenant. Therefore, if Jesus' Name is linked to that Covenant, and that Name can be used to secure the provisions of that Covenant as this passage so clearly teaches, then I have the authority to go after my financial promise using Jesus' Name because finances are promised to me in that Covenant.

For the benefit of those who have not heard this teaching before, God made a Covenant with one man, Abraham, and He promised him some things. He included his seed in those promises. He promised Abraham and his seed healing, prosperity, well being for his family, in addition to salvation for his soul. And you and I, as Gentile Christians, have been grafted into that set of Abrahamic promises; therefore, what was said then applies to you now, because Paul says in Galatians 3 that you and I are the seed of Abraham.

I'm prepared to say to you that there is not one thing missing from the promises God gave Abraham. If that Covenant included healing and prosperity and well being for my family, in addition to the salvation of my soul, I want to ask you a question. What else is there for me to want or need? If I'm sick and I'm promised healing in the Abrahamic Covenant, and God delivers me through the Name of Jesus, that solves that problem. If I'm broke and God promises me prosperity in the Abrahamic Covenant to be secured by using the Name of Jesus, that solves that problem. If I have a problem with one of my family members and God promises me well being for that family member in the Abrahamic Covenant, provided I go at it using the Name of Jesus, does that not also solve that problem? Then what else is there? When you get right down to it, what else is there?

How To Exercise God's Megaton Power Now

What I'm saying to you is that we are authorized as Christians to use the name of Jesus, provided what we use it for is contained in that Abrahamic Covenant. And there is no Jesus, there is no blessing, there is no salvation, there is no healing, there is no prosperity, there is nothing apart from Abraham's Covenant. That is the bedrock of everything.

Have you ever heard a teaching which links the use of Jesus' Name with the healing of the man at the Gate Beautiful to the Abrahamic Covenant? I never have. And yet you can plainly see from the Word of God they are linked together. When you begin to read it and study it you will be amazed at how modern theology has absolutely eliminated the Abrahamic Covenant from their preaching and their teaching and even their believing. It's just not there.

And yet it IS there. Read Acts 3 again, and then read chapter 4. Think it through. You're going to see that the man was healed by Peter using Jesus' Name. You're going to also see that the healing happened in response to the God of Abraham. Now, God only made one deal, and that was with Abraham and his seed. ARE YOU AWARE THAT GOD IS UNDER COVENANT TO NOBODY IN THIS WORLD EXCEPT ABRAHAM AND HIS SEED?

You can talk to me about the New Covenant all day long, and I've heard all the arguments about Old Testament versus New Testamant. But, bless God, the New Testament is nothing more than the ratification of the Abrahamic Covenant by the blood of Jesus Christ. There is ONE covenant that God made with the human race to bless people, and that's the Abrahamic Covenant. And it applies to only one group of people - Abraham and his seed.

But you, Gentile Christians, have been grafted into that system so that everything those Jews were entitled to, you also are now entitled to. If you can get a handle on this it'll make anybody shout - if he's got ears to hear.

The power to get the Abrahamic blessings is contained in the Name of Jesus, because the Name of Jesus operates in and through and because of the Abrahamic Covenant. I challenge you to go back through these

How To Exercise God's Megaton Power Now

Scriptures, I challenge you to look over these Scriptures, I challenge you to read through these Scriptures. There is a link-up between the Name of Jesus and God's Covenant with Abraham. The sooner you see that and know what belongs to you in that Abrahamic Covenant, the sooner you will find yourself with a holy boldness to use the Name of Jesus.

I thank God that I learned two things in my transition out of the denominational church I was in; I learned who I am under the Abrahamic Covenant, and I learned that the Name of Jesus was not just a mental period at the end of a public prayer in a denominational church. The Name of Jesus Christ has power in it, glory to God. And when you learn that the Name works in conjunction with the Abrahamic Covenant and that Covenant covers everything we need, you'll begin to use that Name with boldness. It's not just a cliche, it's not just fine, sweet sounding little theological niceties, but the Name of Jesus Christ will blow the hinges off any door that you need opened. Hallelujah! And it's all linked up to the Abrahamic Covenant.

Let me show you in the Greek text the different ways in which Peter says this man was healed. He said that the man's ankle bones received strength. That is the Greek word "stereao" which is a dead ringer for our English word steroid. The passage also uses the Greek word "eaomai" which always means physical healing. It uses the Greek word "therapeuo" from which comes our word therapeutic. All these words are used to explain how this one man got healed by the use of Jesus' Name based on the Abrahamic Covenant. Twice Peter said that the man was made whole. "Made whole" comes from the Greek word "sozo" from which comes our English word saved. Saved in the Greek text contains healing. Why shouldn't it? It's based on the Abrahamic Covenant and that contains healing.

There is a great problem in today's teaching and preaching. Healing and prosperity have been eliminated from it, but it's because the Abrahamic Covenant is not being taught and preached. But when you put that Abrahamic Covenant back in your theology, you're going to find that healing and prosperity never was eliminated from it. It's all included in the term salvation or saved.

How To Exercise God's Megaton Power Now

My wife and I were in a restaurant the other day, and there was a lady in there who wanted me to pray for her eyes. We went outside in the parking lot on the edge of one of the busiest streets in that area with cars going up and down on both sides. I laid hands on that woman and prayed for her, and began to use the Name of Jesus. When the Name of Jesus began to hit that woman things began to change in her system. When we finished her eyes were not hurting.

I prayed for a lady with lupus, whose back was almost eaten up with that disease. She wanted to be prayed for because she was hurting. I laid hands on her and began to use the Name of Jesus over her; and the Name of Jesus began to bombard the cells, and nerves, and bones and cartilage in that woman's back. She began to straighten up and said, "The pain in my back is easing up." I asked her, "On a scale of one to ten, if you were hurting at a ten when I started, how much are you hurting now?" She answered, "No more than five."

I prayed for her again; I think I prayed for her three times because I don't get embarrassed. Brother, it's God's Word, not mine. I'm not on the spot one bit. He said it, I didn't. I just preach it and do what He says. And if it doesn't work, bless God, we'll all quit this mess, get out of here, and go make some money! But, bless God, IT DOES WORK! So, I laid hands on her again, and she began to straighten up some more. She said, "It's feeling better by the minute. I said, "On a scale of one to ten, where is it now?" She answered, "No more than two." I talked to her sister-in-law the next day, and she reported to me that the woman felt so good, that she was in the kitchen baking, something she had not been able to do in a long while. The sister-in-law said, "You're healing is holding." And I said, "Well, honey, it's not my healing; that's why it's holding." It's the Name of Jesus!

Modern theology, even full gospel theology, pulls all this stuff right out of its context and isolates it. I liken the Word of God to a pearl necklace. Every verse is a pearl. If you clip the string the pearls fall to the floor and roll around at random and come out in a different order than they were. They're still pearls, but they're not in order. All the Bible is composed of pearls. The Abrahamic Covenant is the string upon which the pearls are strung. This gives order to the whole thing. If you clip the string and remove it you still have pearls, but those pearls are jumbled. They are no longer in their order.

How To Exercise God's Megaton Power Now

Again, modern preaching and teaching, even full gospel preaching and teaching, does not see the fact that the Abrahamic Covenant is embedded as deep in Scripture as it actually is. When you begin to read Acts 3 and 4 and see exactly what Peter is saying and see how God honors the Name of His Son, Jesus, you will begin to see that you can use the Name of Jesus to receive any provision contained in the Abrahamic Covenant that belongs to you. And when you really see it you won't be timid in using that Name.

There was a time, even as a Baptist preacher, I was not bold in using the Name of Jesus. I was never personally timid about anything in my life, but I was timid about the Name of Jesus. I never thought it was much more than a cliche. Therefore, it didn't hold much power for me because I'd never been taught about it. But the farther I go in my walk with God, the bolder I get. I will absolutely charge hell with a squirt gun in the Name of Jesus if the Holy Ghost tells me to do it. I've learned that there is power in the Name of Jesus. And it doesn't bother me to pray for cancer any more than for a common cold, because the Name of Jesus is bigger than any other name you can name - whether it's lupus, cancer, AIDS, or the sneezes. The Name of Jesus is THE NAME that is above every name, whether that name is in heaven, on earth, or underneath the earth. I'm telling you, the Name of Jesus can get the job done. And it's all linked up to the Abrahamic Covenant. I'm so happy that God showed me that. I'm so happy that God showed me how to use the Name of Jesus, and I want to share it with you.

I want to challenge you, I want to motivate you, I want you to get bold and brassy, in your use of the Name of Jesus, because there is a lot of evil that's triumphing in the world today. And it's happening because God's people either don't understand the power in Jesus' Name, or if they do they're scared to unleash it. I'm saying that it's time for you to do battle with some of these ungodly strongholds and knock them down using the Name of Jesus. Look at the first part of Acts 3. You won't find Peter praying - not even in the Jesus' Name. He issued it as a command. He told the man, "In the Name of Jesus, get up and walk!"

There's a time to pray, and there's a time to tell the devil what to do in the name of Jesus. Sometimes I'll pray, but sometimes I won't. Sometimes I'll turn the big guns right in the face of the disease and say, "In the Name of Jesus Christ I command you to die, dry up at the roots, and come out of this body." This is what Peter did. There's not one word in these Scriptures that says he prayed one word. I firmly believe that Peter was already prayed up, but I believe that he prayed himself up for himself and not for that man.

And if you're already prayed up, you can do the same thing when called upon by the Spirit of God to do so. Then Peter reached down and grabbed that lame man by the right hand, jerked him, made him stand on his feet, and the man began to jump up and down and leap dance and went into the temple with them. It happened because of who he was - the seed of Abraham. And the Name of Jesus linked to that Covenant gave that man what belonged to him to start with.

The revelation of this is going to give you a wildness about your Christianity you never had before. I want to see a bunch of people who are not scared of anything because they have the most awesome weapon there is at their disposal - THE NAME OF JESUS CHRIST. Is it any wonder that those old prophets that Peter talked about here, as they looked down the corridors of time, could say, "No weapon formed against thee shall prosper."

Listen, I've had people form weapons against me, but they have not prospered yet. They have formed all kinds of weapons against me, but the Word of God says that no weapon formed against me is going to prosper, because I'm right in the middle of that Abrahamic Covenant and I have the Name of Jesus. NO weapon formed against thee shall prosper. I don't have to fear what man can do to me; I have Jesus' Name. I don't have to fear what Satan can do to me; I have Jesus' Name. I don't have to fear what demons can do to me; I have Jesus' Name. And through the use of that Name linked up with the Abrahamic Covenant, we are more than conquerors.

We have Covenant and Name linked up in one chapter as the reason for one man's healing. How plain can you get? Someone can say, "Well, the Abrahamic Covenant is Old Testament." Baloney! I just read it out of the New Testament. Acts 3 is not Old Testament. To relate this back to the Old Testament is foolish! The Abrahamic Covenant is NOW!

If you keep dividing up the pearls of the Word of God - you pick up the Name of Jesus pearl, you pick up the Abrahamic Covenant pearl, then you pick up some other little pearl, and keep them all separated so they cannot come back in their proper order like they should have been before the string was cut - you've still got pearls, but you have robbed yourself of the power in those pearls. Keep all the pearls on the string of the Abrahamic Covenant in their proper order, and you'll find yourself operating in more power than you thought possible. And it's the Name of Jesus that will activate it in your behalf.

In the next chapter we demonstrate from scripture that Jesus' Name will procure for you everything that you will ever need. You will see that this main instrument of God's power, Jesus' Name, will come through for you. You will see that it will secure for you and your family everything contained in The Abrahamic Covenant.

The Main Instrument of Megaton Power And How You Can Use It Now

CHAPTER 5

Proof That Jesus' Name Delivers Everything You Will Ever Need

In this chapter I want to demonstrate some things that the Name of Jesus was used to procure - all of which are in keeping with God's Covenant with Abraham. This Covenant includes healing, prosperity, well being for your family members, in addition to the salvation of your soul. That being the case, since Jesus' Name is linked directly to that Abrahamic Covenant, we need to see other ways in the New Testament in which the Name of Jesus is used to procure the Abrahamic Covenant. In other words, if the Name of Jesus is linked to that Covenant, then I should be able to use His Name to receive healing, prosperity, the well being for every member of my family, as well as the salvation of my soul. I should also be able to use the Name of Jesus to beat off that which hinders me from appropriating and having and achieving and receiving the things that God promised me in that Abrahamic Covenant. Now if the Name of Jesus is linked to that Covenant, it's linked. If it's not, it's not. But if it is, bless God, we need to see it, and we need to see exactly how the Name of Jesus is used in conjunction with the promises of God in that Covenant.

What I want to accomplish in this chapter is to build your faith so that you understand what you have to do when the battle is on. You can read books and listen to sermons that make you feel good, but if you don't learn how to stand in the trenches when the devil's banging you or a member of your family over the head then nobody has done you one bit of good. So what I'm trying to do is equip you. If you'll listen to me you'll have a chance to learn and therefore be equipped when the Devil comes and camps on your front porch, because I'm telling you that if, in fact, you attempt to walk with God you can bet the Devil is going to come see you right where you live.

If you have to always run to me or someone else to pray for you all the time, I've not done my job. What I've got to do is teach you what belongs to you and teach you how to get it by helping you to get the weapons of God's warfare in your hands. If I can do that, you'll change from someone who only wants to belong to a "bless me club" into someone who can stand up in the trenches, look the devil right in the face, and tell him to go straight to hell where he belongs. But until I can teach you to do that, I really have not done my job. So, I'm going to teach - what you do with it is up to you.

Having said all that, let's take a look at some uses of the Name of Jesus. Read the following verses of scripture from Acts 16:

> Acts 16:16-19
> 16 And it came to pass, as we went to prayer, a certain damsel possessed with a spirit of divination met us, which brought her masters much gain by soothsaying:
> 17 The same followed Paul and us, and cried, saying, These men are the servants of the most high God, which shew unto us the way of salvation.
> 18 And this did she many days. But Paul, being grieved, turned and said to the spirit, I command thee in the name of Jesus Christ to come out of her. And he came out the same hour.
> 19 And when her masters saw that the hope of their gains was gone, they caught Paul and Silas, and drew them into the marketplace unto the rulers,

How To Exercise God's Megaton Power Now

Now here is a demon possessed girl, and this demon in her had the ability to foretell something that was going to happen; she had a spirit of divination (soothsaying, fortune telling). Some people think that a lot of this fortune telling stuff is fake. A lot of it is, but a lot of it is real. There are demons that can actually do that. This girl had a demon that could foretell the future, and this girl brought her owners, her masters, much gain by functioning as a fortune teller. Undoubtedly, she had great success at it because she brought MUCH gain to her owners; she had probably built up a repeat business.

We now see psychics advertising on television all the time now. They get all these silly movie stars on stage to "testify" about this great psychic who helped them do this, that, and the other. And the question is, "Can they do it?" Those psychics can't, but the demons that inhabit them can. Therefore, there is validity to it. This is exactly what is happening right here in verse 16. Paul met this girl who was demon possessed with a spirit of divination, which enabled her to tell fortunes.

Now look at verses 17 and 18. Here is one way to use Jesus' Name, and it's done by a member of the Abrahamic Seed Group - Paul. There is nothing to indicate that girl was saved. As a matter of fact, she probably was not even a Jew but a Gentile. That girl was demon possessed and not saved. But Paul saw that in order to free her of that demon and get her saved, he was going to have to exorcize that demon spirit. How did he do it? He placed a command on that demon using the Name of Jesus, and the demon was forced to obey what Paul said.

I have seen many problems between people, and they relate these problems to personality clashes or differences of opinion or differences of religion or this or that. When all the while the problem is demonic and has nothing to do with personality or religion or anything else. Until a child of God, a seed of Abraham, recognizes that some things are of a spirit nature and recognizes that through the use of Jesus' Name they have power over that spirit world, they are never going to get to the bottom of their problem.

I have seen marriages end in divorce, not because of the man or the woman, but as a result of demonic activity in their marriage. They did not understand what was happening, and so ended up in divorce court. If only they could have gotten around somebody who had the spiritual vision to penetrate and see what the problem was and deal with the problem (which was a demon) using Jesus' Name.

Now learn something. Paul is a member of the Abrahamic Seed Group. (If you're saved, you're also a member of the Abrahamic Seed Group.) What is Paul doing here in Acts 16? He was authorized and empowered by God to use the Name of Jesus over that girl and command that demon to come out of her, and verse 18 says that it came out the same hour. So then I, as a member of the Abrahamic Seed Group, have the same authority.

Mark 16 gives me the authority to use Jesus' Name over demonic activity and force it to do what I tell it to do. The next time some of this mess hits you or someone you love, you can try all the world's ways of solving it. But until you come to grips with the fact that this just might be the result of demonic activity and exercise the Name of Jesus over the situation, you run the great risk of losing it all. There is only one power that the demon will heed to. You cannot coerce him out, you cannot coax him out, you cannot force him out, you cannot do anything to get him out except **command** him in the Name of Jesus. THAT he listens to. According to Mark 16, every Christian, every member of the Abrahamic Seed Group has that authority.

Is there a problem in your life, especially if it pertains to another person? Have you ever stopped to consider the fact that there just might be a demonic cause to the problem? If it is demonic, why are you trying to solve it some other way? You may sugarcoat it, butter it up, cover it up, and play like it's not a demon problem. But that thing can hide and con you into believing that it's gone, then six months down the road it will manifest itself, and then what are you going to do?

You need to get on top of this and recognize demonic forces now. You need to understand that the only power that will ever make that thing leave is the power in the Name of Jesus. This authority is given ONLY to the Abrahamic Seed Group, and if you are Abraham's seed (and you are if you're saved), you have that power and authority right now. USE IT!

How To Exercise God's Megaton Power Now

We do have power over demons, but let me insert some caution right here. If you have never gotten close enough to God and deep enough in the Word to settle the fact that you actually do have the power to command demons, then you had better not try to do it until you GET close enough in your walk with God and deep enough in the Word so that your mind is renewed by the Word and you KNOW who you are and what your rights are. Until you get to that point, you better leave demons alone, because they will turn on you and attack you. Let me show you a case of that in the Bible:

> Acts 19:13-20
> 13 Then certain of the vagabond Jews, exorcists, took upon them to call over them which had evil spirits the name of the Lord Jesus, saying, We adjure you by Jesus whom Paul preacheth.
> 14 And there were seven sons of one Sceva, a Jew, and chief of the priests, which did so.
> 15 And the evil spirit answered and said, Jesus I know, and Paul I know; but who are ye?
> 16 And the man in whom the evil spirit was leaped on them, and overcame them, and prevailed against them, so that they fled out of that house naked and wounded.
> 17 And this was known to all the Jews and Greeks also dwelling at Ephesus; and fear fell on them all, and the name of the Lord Jesus was magnified.
> 18 And many that believed came, and confessed, and shewed their deeds.
> 19 Many of them also which used curious arts brought their books together, and burned them before all men: and they counted the price of them, and found it fifty thousand pieces of silver.
> 20 So mightily grew the word of God and prevailed.

How To Exercise God's Megaton Power Now

Acts 19:13 says "certain of the vagabond Jews...." - not saved people, but vagabond, reprobate Jews; people who were in religion for money - "exorcists, took upon them to call over them which had evil spirits the name of the Lord Jesus, saying, We adjure you by Jesus whom Paul preacheth." Now, get a handle on that. You think that's not an anemic, cop-out approach! "I'm so unsure of myself, and I don't have guts enough to stand flat footed and tell that thing what to do in Jesus' Name. So I'm going to adjure you by Jesus whom Paul preaches." Come on!

These guys KNEW they didn't have the authority to use Jesus' Name. Notice what happened in the verse 14. Now, this guy was the top dog religious leader. He was the chief of the priests, but he didn't know WHO he was, if he was even saved. He certainly had no confidence. If he knew anything about the Name of Jesus, he really didn't have confidence that it would work for him. Look at verse 15. Yeah, sure - "I adjure you by the Jesus that Paul preacheth." He didn't say HE preached Him. That's the tragedy in preaching from the Saturday Evening Post, the Reader's Digest, and the newspaper. You keep your people informed, but there is no power in your preaching.

I remember years ago when a large denomination had a training union. In 1970 when they changed the curriculum, they gutted it, and they have never been the same. I don't say that to be ugly, but, they changed the content and the approach to the old training union and began to teach and preach the social gospel. They wrecked the greatest thing in that denomination, which was the training that taught their people to do what they do today.

Sceva and his sons did not know who they were. They had no concept of the power of the Name of Jesus. I'm convinced from reading these Scriptures that they really had no concept of who Jesus Himself was. Brother, I don't want to preach the Jesus that somebody else preaches. I want to preach the Jesus that I preach, the Jesus that I personnally know. When you start walking with God to the point where you can begin to couple your own experiences to Scripture and you preach that, then you'll have a platform and a power to launch out from that will change the entire world around you! Because people will respond to a man who knows who he is and knows what he's talking about.

How To Exercise God's Megaton Power Now

When YOUR lifestyle and your life experiences can be coupled to Scripture and you're standing up preaching what you KNOW to be the truth, people WILL respond because they can TELL you KNOW. People want to hear somebody who knows that they know that they know! And this business of "I preach Jesus whom Paul preached" is nonsense. When you begin to test the waters and stand on your own experience with God, you know what you're talking about, because you've tried it and proved it. Hallelujah!

But, when your life experiences are so shallow in the things of God, everybody around you will know how anemic you really are as a Christian. You may give lip service, like Sceva and his boys, but that won't hack it, for when people hear you, they will spot you for what you are - very inexperienced! I can be around a person three minutes and listen to them pray, and I can tell you exactly where that man or woman is on the scales of God Almighty, because they pray based on experience linked up with the Scripture. When I hear somebody pray this "Now I lay me down to sleep, I pray the Lord my soul to keep" type prayer, I know that their experience with God does not go beyond the nursery. Nobody is going to listen to them. They are the ones that come up with this "I adjure thee by the Jesus that Paul preaches" stuff. Do you want to know what happens to this type of person? Look at verse 16. That never would have happened if Sceva had not come at that thing with second hand information.

Listen, when you've tested the waters yourself, and you've walked a little way with God, and you've found that your experiences match up with the Word of God, that'll take you out of the nursery and turn you into a man or woman of God. You'll learn to trust your own experiences, because your experience with God matches up with the Word of God, and it gives you a fire and a boldness and holy guts. I dare a demon to jump in my face! You just watch what I do to him; I'll turn that little punk every way but loose in the Name of Jesus. Why? Because I know who I am, I've tested the Name of Jesus, and I know the power in that Name over any demon or any other name, whether it's in heaven, hell, or earth. I'm not scared.

There was a time when I was scared because I didn't know anything. I got my initiation into this demon stuff as a Baptist evangelist. I was

How To Exercise God's Megaton Power Now

in a meeting in Memphis, Tennessee one night, and this crazy, wild-eyed, fireball Baptist pastor of the church scared the daylights out of me. I thought, "My God, where on the surface of this globe am I? This cannot possibly be a Baptist church. I do believe that I am in the inside of the biggest, craziest asylum that ever has been erected on God's green earth!" I thought this because one night this pastor said to me, "I want you to come with me to my office. I want to show you something." I was already leery, because I was scared of this guy.

I asked him, "What are you going to show me?" He said, "I'm going to show you a demon possessed man, and we're going to cast the demons out of him." I said to myself, "Oh, my God! I don't want to see this." I'd never messed with this kind of stuff. All I knew how to do was preach hell and how to stay out of it. That was the sum total of my theology.

But this crazy Baptist pastor got me in his office, and sure enough there was this guy sitting in a chair who was demonic. As soon as we walked into the office he fell from the chair and began to writher around on the floor like a snake. His body moved and made the turns exactly like a snake crawling across the floor. The voice that came out of that man was a totally different voice from what is normal for a human being.

I experienced something that I'd never seen before, because when that man was under the influence of that demon, he had super-human strength. He crawled across the floor towards the wall, and when he reached it, he locked his finger nails behind the baseboard of that wall, pulled it off the wall, and splintered it into a thousand pieces with just his fingers. The pastor had a handmade oak desk that weighed at least 200 pounds. At that time I weighed over 200 pounds, but I was sitting behind that desk - and I was glad of it. I sure didn't want to be out in the middle of the floor.

Anyway, I was leaning on that desk when all of a sudden he started crawling towards the desk. I said to myself, "Oh, my Father, make that guy crawl toward the other end of this room!" Meanwhile, the pastor is dealing with that demon, and the guy is talking in this weird voice, and he's getting closer and closer to me. He finally made it to the edge of the desk. Still laying flat on the floor, he grabbed one leg of the desk with one hand; and remember, I'm weighing in at 200 pounds leaning over the desk that weighs at least 200 pounds. That's a minimum of 400 pounds. This guy, in a position in which it is impossible to get any leverage, shoved that 200 pound desk and my 200 pound body up into the air and against the back wall.

But, thank God, that crazy Baptist pastor was not a son of Sceva! He knew what to do, and he had everything under control. He delivered that man from the power of the demon, and that demon didn't leap out on anybody including me, because that pastor wouldn't let him. This was my first experience with demons. But listen, the Name of Jesus Christ freed that man right there on the spot, with me sitting there looking at it saying, "Thank You, God!"

The point is this. You've got to know who you are, you've got to know the power in the Name of Jesus, and you've got to know that the power is yours. You've got to start out somewhere walking with God. You can't get all this experience in the classroom or in Bible Study. You've got to start walking it out. If you'll start, you're going to find, bits and pieces at a time, that this actually works! And as you learn that this stuff actually works, it will motivate you to get braver and stronger; and you'll learn to deal with every problem by looking it right in the face, using the Name of Jesus on it, and making the demon do what you tell it to. So, if you are a member of this Abrahamic Seed Group, you have the power and authority to tell a demon exactly what to do. But if you're a son of Sceva, you need to walk way around the other way.

In Acts 3 after Peter and John had healed the lame man at the Gate Beautiful, the religious leadership of the day got so bent out of shape they could hardly stand themselves. Now look at Acts 4:13-21. __

> Acts 4:13-21
> 13 Now when they saw the boldness of Peter and John, and perceived that they were unlearned and ignorant men, they marvelled; and they took knowledge of them, that they had been with Jesus.
> 14 And beholding the man which was healed standing with them, they could say

nothing against it.

15 But when they had commanded them to go aside out of the council, they conferred among themselves,

16 Saying, What shall we do to these men? for that indeed a notable miracle hath been done by them is manifest to all them that dwell in Jerusalem; and we cannot deny it.

17 But that it spread no further among the people, let us straitly threaten them, that they speak henceforth to no man in this name.

18 And they called them, and commanded them not to speak at all nor teach in the name of Jesus.

19 But Peter and John answered and said unto them, Whether it be right in the sight of God to hearken unto you more than unto God, judge ye.

20 For we cannot but speak the things which we have seen and heard.

21 So when they had further threatened them, they let them go, finding nothing how they might punish them, because of the people: for all men glorified God for that which was done.

22 For the man was above forty years old, on whom this miracle of healing was shewed.

That bunch of religious people quickly learned the power in the Name of Jesus, because it was the Name of Jesus that Peter and John used to get that lame man healed in Chapter 3, and it just blew their religious minds. I mean, here are two men who stood flat footed, used the name of a man who was supposedly dead, and said, "In the Name of Jesus, I command you to rise and walk", and the man did. Brother, the word spread! So they told Peter and John, "We don't want you to speak or teach any more in that Name." Now, look at Acts 4:23-31.

How To Exercise God's Megaton Power Now

Acts 4:23-31

23 And being let go, they went to their own company, and reported all that the chief priests and elders had said unto them.

24 And when they heard that, they lifted up their voice to God with one accord, and said, Lord, thou art God, which hast made heaven, and earth, and the sea, and all that in them is:

25 Who by the mouth of thy servant David hast said, Why did the heathen rage, and the people imagine vain things?

26 The kings of the earth stood up, and the rulers were gathered together against the Lord, and against his Christ.

27 For of a truth against thy holy child Jesus, whom thou hast anointed, both Herod, and Pontius Pilate, with the Gentiles, and the people of Israel, were gathered together,

28 For to do whatsoever thy hand and thy counsel determined before to be done.

29 And now, Lord, behold their threatenings: and grant unto thy servants, that with all boldness they may speak thy word,

30 By stretching forth thine hand to heal; and that signs and wonders may be done by the name of thy holy child Jesus.

31 And when they had prayed, the place was shaken where they were assembled together; and they were all filled with the Holy Ghost, and they spake the word of God with boldness.

In verse 29 and 30 they ask God for **boldness to speak** the word and for **signs and wonders to be done** by the Name of Jesus. Listen, the signs and wonders are waiting on somebody who has enough audacity to use the Name of Jesus. The more I learn to use the Name of Jesus, the more convinced I am in the power of it. I have seen things happen as a result of using His Name that absolutely blows the mind. I have seen signs and wonders take place in my own life that absolutely would never have occurred outside of using that Name.

You can use the Name of Jesus, if you are a member of the Abrahamic Seed Group, to procure those things promised by God to that Seed Group. Genesis 22:18 is a direct linkage between healing and the Abrahamic Covenant, the person of Jesus and the Name of Jesus.

> Gen 22:18
> 18 And in thy seed shall all the nations of the earth be blessed; because thou hast obeyed my voice.

Do you need a miracle in your life? Then the Name of Jesus is the way to see it happen. You can sit around, wish and hope and pray, but there comes a time when you must use the Name of Jesus to make the miracle happen. I don't know about you, but I like living in a realm of signs and wonders. My whole life is a sign and wonder. Ever since I've been in the ministry, my whole ministry has hung by a thread. It's a sign and a wonder that I'm able preach at all.

I give God Almighty praise for the Name of Jesus, for I have used that Name to beat off the attacks of the devil for so many years that it's automatic. I do it under my breath without thinking about it. My mind is so renewed to the use of Jesus' Name, because apart from that Name I'd be out of the ministry - in fact, I never would have started. If you only knew the depth of what I'm driving at you would understand that I am the greatest sign and wonder you've ever seen, because right after God called me to preach everything in this world blew up in my face. And it's never really landed outright yet, but by the power of God Almighty I am what I am. Were it not for the Name of Jesus this ministry would terminate before this night was over. But because of that Name nothing will stop it, Hallelujah!

So, if the miracle that you need is contained any where in the perimeters of that Abrahamic Covenant, bless God, you can spring the Name of Jesus on it and force the circumstances to line up the way you want it.

How To Exercise God's Megaton Power Now

We've talked about signs and wonders, the healing of the lame man in Acts 3, and demons being subject to Jesus' Name. Now let me show you one more thing. I want to show you the power of the Name over things. There may be things that come against you, things and circumstances that the devil engineers and throws at you, things that try to hinder the will of God for your life. And I want to show you the power of Jesus' Name over these things. Look at John 14:13,

> John 14:13
> 13 And whatsoever ye shall <u>ask</u> in my name, that will I do, that the Father may be glorified in the Son.

Look at the word "ask". Greeks had more than one word for ask. They had the regular word for ask, then they had another word which meant ask in as strong a manner as possible. The word "ask" that is used in this Scripture is the Greek word AITEO, which literally means not only ask in as strong a manner as possible, but the basic meaning of that word is to issue a command, to ASK something in the form of a COMMAND. If I say to someone, "Give me $10.00 quickly!", I'm asking, but at the same time, I'm asking so strongly that it's a command. Do you see this? Let me take this a step further.

When that word is used in conjunction with a thing it should be translated "command". If that word happens to be used in conjunction with God, we don't command God, but we strongly ask. Can you see the difference? Here in John 14:13 it's used in conjunction with a thing; therefore, we are to translate the word as "command" not "ask". Look at the Scripture again. Jesus says, "Whatsoever....". That's a thing. So we can translate this verse, "Whatsoever you command in my name, that will I do...."

So then, if I as am a member of the Abrahamic Seed Group, am confronted by a thing that get's between me and what God promised me in that Abrahamic Covenant, I am authorized to issue a command to that thing using the Name of Jesus. I can do that because Jesus is the 60th promise of Genesis 22:18. He is the seed of Genesis 22:18. Remember, through the Name of Jesus linked to the Abrahamic Covenant, the lame man at the gate was healed of his sickness. Is sickness a thing? Yes, it is.

How To Exercise God's Megaton Power Now

So, if a thing confronts me in such a way that it is going to prevent me from having what's mine in the Abrahamic Covenant, I am authorized by the Son of God to issue a command using the Name of Jesus, and guess who is going to carry out that command that I issue? Jesus said that He would do it! I don't know about you brother, but when Jesus is on the scene I feel pretty secure. If Jesus said that He was the one who was going to make good on it, I feel pretty good about what He said, because He has the integrity to keep His word. I am sure also, that He has the power to pull off whatever He said He was going to do.

When Jesus said, "If you make a command on a whatsoever or a thing, I'm the One who's going to do it, provided you command the thing in My Name." What am I authorized to command in His Name? Anything that He Himself would command to start with, I can command. If it's in that Abrahamic Covenant I have the authority to issue a command on any "whatsoever" that get's in the way of me realizing what is mine in that Covenant.

When a "whatsoever" or a "thing" comes your way, and you begin to see that this "thing" is going to try to stop you from having what God has promised, issue a command to that thing in the Name of Jesus and tell that "thing" to get out of your face! Make it shift it's gear, turn around, and go some other direction.

"WHATSOEVER you command in my name," Jesus said, "I will do it." Is this power or not? Listen, you better recognize and learn that as a Christian the only source of help you've got is supernatural, because there is nothing in this world you can really rely upon except the Name of Jesus. When you get that down deep-seeded in your spirit you can do business with God.

Start walking it out. All this head knowledge is junk! I know a man still in his twenties, who has memorized the entire Bible. You can start any verse of Scripture, give him two or three words, and he can pick it up, finish quoting it, and tell you where it's found in the Bible. But the man has no power, it's all head knowledge. His mind is not renewed. He has no experience with God. He's not tested it on the anvil of experience.

How To Exercise God's Megaton Power Now

I'm simply saying to you, don't be like the sons of Sceva and say, "I adjure you by the Jesus Paul preaches." Brother, sister, you've got to do adjuring by the Jesus you know, and you've got to test it out by walking it out. When you do you're life will change, and you will not be one of those who has to call on someone else to pray for you every time you sneeze. You'll get into the praying business for other people that sneeze. It's the Name of Jesus linked to the Covenant that contains the power.

From the very beginning of my ministry I was forced to find God. I am absolutely driven to God. When you're forced to rely upon something or somebody greater than yourself, it'll do something to you. But when all is said and done it will give you a character and depth that will stand and face any storm, for you KNOW the Name of Jesus can silence the storm. All Jesus has to do is say to the storm, "Peace, be still", and the storms in your life will calm.

You MUST learn to use the Name of Jesus, because the days are coming when you may not have somebody to call on to pray for you. The heat is going to be on, and you're going to HAVE to learn to stand on your own. The guy who has head knowledge only will be first to buckle, because he'll sell out and go by the wayside.

Thank God for the Name of Jesus. He has a Name that's above every name. It doesn't matter what gets thrown in my face, I have a Name with power that's greater than anything. I have the same power, and the same great Name that Peter had. That name will do for me what it did for Peter. It will do it for you too. It is yours. Use it!

In the next section (five chapters) we learn that the same holiness that Peter drew from in the healing of the lame man is our holiness also. This is seen under the heading *God's Five Bedrock Foundations of Megaton Power and How You Can Stand On Them.*

People Across The Country Are Saying:

The Most Life Changing Thing Ever Written On Healing And Prosperity Are The Author's Four Books On The Abrahamic Covenant:

- **What Are Abraham's Blessings Anyway?**

This Volume Explains Why Jesus *MUST Heal* and Prosper You Now.

- **What've They Done With Abraham's Blessings?**

This Volume Destroys The Modernistic Denial That Healing and Prosperity Belong To Christians Now

- **The Unbroken Force of Abraham's Blessings**

The Main Reason To Deny That Healing and Prosperity Belong To Christians Now, Defined, Examined, Refuted and Destroyed

- **How To Obtain Abraham's Blessings**

A Simple, Step by Step Guide To Obtaining The Healing, Prosperity and Well-being For Every Member of Your Family That God Promised You in The Abrahamic Covenant.

These Four Books Will Build Your Faith To A Fever Pitch. Order Yours Now, Here, Today. You'll Be Glad You Did!

The Five Bedrock Foundations of Megaton Power And Why You Can Stand On Them Now

CHAPTER 6

The Two Shocking Accomplishments of The Offering Up Of Jesus' Physical Body and What This Does To Power You Up Now

Hebrews 10:1-23 states that it was the will of God for Jesus to be offered **once** as the **final** sacrifice for **all** of the sins of the world.

> 1   For the law having a shadow of good things to come, and not the very image of the things, can never with those sacrifices which they offered year by year continually make the comers thereunto perfect.
> 2   For then would they not have ceased to be offered? because that the worshippers once purged should have had no more conscience of sins.
> 3   But in those sacrifices there is a remembrance again made of sins every year.
> 4   For it is not possible that the blood of bulls and of goats should take away sins.
> 5   Wherefore when he cometh into the world, he saith, Sacrifice and offering thou wouldest not, but a body hast thou prepared me:

6 In burnt offerings and sacrifices for **sin** thou hast had no pleasure.

7 Then said I, Lo, I come (in the volume of the book it is written of me,) to do thy **will,** O God.

8 Above when he said, Sacrifice and offering and burnt offerings and offering for sin thou wouldest not, neither hadst pleasure therein; which are offered by the law;

9 Then said he, Lo, I come to do thy will, O God. He taketh away the first, that he may establish the second.

10 By the which will we are sanctified through the offering of the body of Jesus Christ once for all.

11 And every priest standeth daily ministering and offering oftentimes the same sacrifices, which can never take away sins:

12 But this man, after he had offered one sacrifice for sins for ever, sat down on the right hand of God;

13 From henceforth expecting till his enemies be made his footstool.

14 For by one offering he hath perfected for ever them that are sanctified.

15 Whereof the Holy Ghost also is a witness to us: for after that he had said before,

16 This is the covenant that I will make with them after those days, saith the Lord, I will put my laws into their hearts, and in their minds will I write them;

17 And their sins and iniquities will I remember no more.

18 Now where remission of these is, there is no more offering for sin.

19 Having therefore, brethren, boldness to enter into the holiest by the blood of Jesus,

20 By a new and living way, which he hath

> consecrated for us, through the veil, that is to say, his flesh;
> 21 And having an high priest over the house of God;
> 22 Let us draw near with a true heart in full assurance of faith, having our hearts sprinkled from an evil conscience, and our bodies washed with pure water.
> 23 Let us hold fast the profession of our faith without wavering; (for he is faithful that promised;)

It was through that one act, the sacrificial death of Christ, that God could separate or sanctify us from the rest of mankind forever. So I'm sanctified by the offering of the body of Christ once for all, verse 10. The word "sanctified" from the Greek text means to separate or to set apart. That sanctification was a one time process when I was set apart by God for His own use.

Notice verse 11, "And every priest standeth daily ministering and offering often the same sacrifices." The writer of the book of Hebrews is contrasting the priesthood of Jesus with the priesthood of Old Testament Judaism. Those priests had to stand daily and offer sacrifices over and over again. Often times, they offered the same sacrifices. The reason they had to do that was because those sacrifices could never take away sin.

There was a difference between the sacrificial system in Moses' law and Abraham's Covenant. Through the Abrahamic Covenant people were granted, by grace, salvation, healing, and prosperity. The law was added to deal with the sin problem and yet enable them to maintain the blessings of Abraham. When they violated a law of Moses these various sacrifices came into play. They had to make the proper sacrifice so that the blessings of Abraham would stay in effect.

But notice something, the sacrifices they made could never take away their sins. All it could do was cause God to defer judgment on it. For all the Old Testament sins were, at the death of Christ, brought up from past history and placed on the cross, and the blood of Jesus Christ cleansed and took away the sins of all the people in the Old

Testament who had made the proper sacrifice. Since the sacrifices could not take away the sin, but only caused God to defer judgment on it, they had to do it daily.

But now let's contrast that with the blood of Jesus. Contrast what the Old Testament high priest did with what Jesus, our heavenly priest, did. The Bible says that it's the will of God that through the offering of Jesus' body, we are sanctified once for all. The Old Testament priest had to continuously stand daily ministering an offering - the same sacrifices. And those sacrifices could never take away sin.

But this man Jesus, after He had offered one sacrifice for sins forever, sat down on the right hand of God. Those Old Testament priests had to STAND and offer sacrifices daily. Jesus made one sacrifice and then sat down, signifying His work was finished. They had to stand daily and continuously minister and offer sacrifices - the same sacrifices - for the simple reason that those sacrifices never did take away sin. It caused God to wait to judge it, but it never took it away. That's why they had to continuously do it over and over and over again.

But the offering of the body of Jesus Christ was a once-for-all sacrifice. And, it was the will of God that through that one offering sins were taken away and God could sanctify or separate us. To signify that His work is done, there is a place in the throne room of heaven where our high priest can sit down, and He is sitting there right now. But there was no chair in the Holy of Holies in the Old Testament temple. There was no place for that high priest to sit down, because his work was never finished. What he did could never permanently sanctify or set apart those people. But since the offering of Jesus' body was a once for all offering and a finished work, why not sit down? When you finish something, what do you do? You sit down. Sitting down signifies that the job is over.

So here it is - one offering, finished job, sitting down, sanctified. What is He doing now? Verse 13 tells us:
> 13 From henceforth expecting till his enemies be made his footstool.

He is sitting at the right hand of the Father in anticipation, waiting for the time, till his enemies be made his footstool. The day is coming when the enemies of Jesus Christ are going to be trampled under His feet. That's not happening yet, but it's coming. Listen, let me tell you something. The day is coming in this country when it's going to cost you to name the Name of Christ, because there are enemies to the cross of Jesus in this land. It's going to get worse and worse. Jesus is sitting in heaven anticipating the day when He can come back and deal with His enemies, putting them under His feet, and turning them into His footstool.

Look at verse 10 and 14.

> 10 By the which will we are sanctified through the offering of the body of Jesus Christ once for all.
> 14 For by one offering he hath perfected for ever them that are sanctified.

Notice in verse 10 that it says we are "sanctified" through the offering of His body. So since we are sanctified by that one offering, He has "perfected" us forever, verse 14. The word "perfected" in this Scripture does not have the same meaning in English today as when it was written. The Scripture that says, "Be ye therefore perfect....", does not mean the same thing today as it did in King James' day. It's a Greek word which means brought to the end of a process.

If something has been brought to the end of a process it means that there is no more developmental change that is possible; therefore, we can say it's perfect. The average Christian reads "Be ye therefore perfect....", throws his hands up, and says, "I CAN'T BE PERFECT!" But the word "perfect" means brought to the end of a process, or completion. What this says is that by that offering we are sanctified. Since we ARE sanctified He's perfected us. That is, He has brought us to the very end of all the process and into a state of completion. There is no more that God or we can do to make us perfect. Jesus has done it all.

The devil will play games with us. He'll make Scriptures say things that they don't really mean and make you get under a guilt trip. The devil says, "You're not perfect." But the Bible says that Jesus HAS perfected us. So if the devil says that you're not perfected, but the

How To Exercise God's Megaton Power Now

Bible says that you are, who are you going to believe? The devil comes back and tells me that I'm not perfected, I'm going right back in his face and say, "I'm perfected." He says, "No, you're not perfected." I'm going to say, "The Bible says that I'm perfected." He says, "You can't possibly be perfected, look at you." I'm going to say to him, "The Bible says that I'm perfected." I'm going with the Word no matter what the devil or anybody else has to say about it. I am perfected through the offering of the body of Jesus Christ.

There is a sense in which we need to sanctify ourselves. And there is a sense in which we do. But in this passage, we HAVE been sanctified by the sacrifice of Jesus. God does the sanctifying because of the offering of the body of Christ. So what we need to do is pick up two confessions. We need to say, "I'm sanctified." Secondly, we need to say, "I'm perfected." Every time the devil throws something at you, you need to hit him right back with Scripture exactly like Jesus did. In Matthew 4 when Jesus was led into the wilderness to be tempted by the devil, He quoted him Scripture.

So we need to say, "I'm sanctified. I'm perfected." When the devil comes to you and plays you some old tapes about stuff you did, you need to play him a tape or two. The tapes need to say over and over again, "I'm sanctified, I'm perfected! I'm sanctified, I'm perfected! I'm sanctified, I'm perfected!" In neither of these confessions, however, am I the one doing the action. I'm "receiving" the actions, I'm "receiving" the perfection, and I'm "receiving" the sanctification, because it was something God did TO me through the offering of the body of Jesus.

When you see and understand who the Bible says you are and begin to SAY what the Bible says you are, you're faith will begin to wind up like a spring. It will be built up to fever pitch. Brother, according to the Word of Almighty God, I have been sanctified, I have been perfected, I am everything that God wants me to be. And if there is anything lacking, God will work it in me, because Philippians 1:6 says,

> 6 Being confident of this very thing, that he which hath begun a good work in you will perform it until the day of Jesus Christ:

So if there IS anything lacking God will take care of that also. When the devil comes at you, he's insulting the high priesthood of Jesus. He's saying that the offering of Jesus' body was not sufficient for you - YOU must do more. However, if I am already sanctified and perfected by God Himself, and Jesus did the job so well that He sat down and has done nothing else to make me more perfect, why should I worry about it? Believe that you are who the Bible says you are, open your mouth and begin to confess who you are, and the devil will flee from you just like he did from Jesus. When I get down and discouraged the best way to beat those feelings is to start saying what the Scripture says about me.

There is something about the spirit inside you that will tell you when you're on the right track and when you're not.

> Heb 10:15-17
> 15 Whereof the Holy Ghost also is a witness to us: for after that he had said before,
> 16 This is the covenant that I will make with them after those days, saith the Lord, I will put my laws into their hearts, and in their minds will I write them;
> 17 And their sins and iniquities will I remember no more.

As illogical as it sounds, when you begin to confess, "I am sanctified and perfected," there is an inner witness in you that will agree, "You're right, you are." Now your mind will remind you about what you did today, "You got mad as fire over this thing. You wanted to cuss the cat and kick the dog. Look at what you did!" But, bless God, you are perfected, and you are sanctified, and the Holy Ghost witnesses, "Yes, you are!"

The Holy Ghost is a witness to us. I learned this about the Holy Ghost right after I got saved. I found myself in the hardest, toughest book in the Bible, Romans, two days after I was saved. I found the passage that says, "The Spirit Himself beareth witness with us that we are the sons of God...." And when I read that something begin to well up inside me, and I KNEW that I was a son of God. There was an inner knowing, a witness inside me that said, "You are a son of God."

Anytime you confess the Word, even if that Word seems illogical to the natural mind (because most of the Word does seem illogical to the natural mind), there will be a witness inside you that it is so. Brother, I'm sanctified, I'm perfected. And there is a witness inside me that says, "That's right."

Look at verse 16 again.

> HEB. 10:16-17
> 16 This is the covenant that I will make with them after those days, saith the Lord, I will put my laws into their hearts, and in their minds will I write them;
> 17 And their sins and iniquities will I remember no more.

After what days? After the day that Jesus died, paid for our sins, rose and went into heaven, and sat down. Then there was a new covenant to be made; not new in time, but new in quality. One aspect of that covenant which we refer to as the New Covenant is this; Jesus obliterated the law of Moses, it no longer exists. Instead of living under that law he said, "I will put my law into their hearts, and in their minds will I write them." He put the entire Scripture in our hearts. So, when you confess the Word, it's that Word that He placed in your heart and wrote in your mind that the Holy Ghost is a witness to. I firmly believe that if a man or woman surrenders to God to the proper degree, when he or she needs a Scripture from anywhere in the Bible, the Holy Ghost will call it up to their memory. This is what Jesus taught in the book of John. He said,

> John 14:26
> 26 But the Comforter, which is the Holy Ghost, whom the Father will send in my name, he shall teach you all things, and bring all things to your remembrance, whatsoever I have said unto you.

How To Exercise God's Megaton Power Now

Jesus said that when the Spirit of truth comes He will call all things to your memory that He has taught. The Holy Ghost, since that time, has placed the laws of God in our hearts and written them in our minds. I have said many times that I never attempt to memorize Scripture. I certainly have no problem with anyone who does, but I have found that the Scripture teaches that when I need to remember something the Holy Ghost will bring me the Scripture. I have never found it to fail.

I have been able to quote Scripture that I have never memorized. The Holy Ghost has given me Greek words, before I ever studied Greek, as I was preaching. After finishing the sermon I would look in my Greek New Testament to see if I had used the right word, and I did! Why did the Holy Ghost do that? That's His job. He puts the Word in our hearts and writes it in our minds, then triggers it, calls it up, and makes us aware of it when we need it. There's an inner knowing, and it's all supernatural.

I received a telephone call from a woman recently who was in such turmoil that she was panicking. She had read something in the Bible that did not apply to her as a Christian, but she had applied it to herself anyway. There were some things that she had done years ago that the devil was throwing in her face and bringing her into condemnation for it. I read I John 1:9 to her,

> I Jn 1:9
> 9   If we confess our sins, he is faithful and just to forgive us our sins, and to cleanse us from all unrighteousness.

But verse 17 in Hebrews 10 goes farther than that.

> Heb. 10:17
> 17   And their sins and iniquities will I remember no more.

Not only does this verse say that He forgives and cleanses, but thank God, He remembers those sins and iniquities no more! When you're walking in the Spirit this is what the Holy Ghost will witness to you. "God doesn't even remember your sin! Why do you keep bringing it up?" In contrast, the witness of the devil and the flesh keeps hounding you with your past. Listen, if we (I mean ALL of us) let the devil hound us over sins of the past - or even sins of today - it will drive us nuts. What we MUST recognize is that the blood of God's Son, Jesus Christ, cleanses and keeps on cleansing (Greek present tense) us from ALL our sins. When He does God does not remember them, and the Holy Ghost will tell you that if you'll get quiet and listen.

Nothing I said seemed to quiet this woman down. I couldn't stop her from going off one wall and onto another. I said, "What you are doing is taking things out of context and making Scripture speak things to you that it is not saying." She asked me, "Well, what about the Spirit of God leaving King Saul?" I said, "You're not King Saul! He's not a Christian even to this hour, and you are. Do you remember the Philippian jailer who asked Paul, 'What must I do to be saved?' What if somebody pulled out the Scripture about Judas hanging himself right here and responded with that Scripture to the Philippian jailer, 'Go out and hang yourself!' It's taken out of context. It doesn't make any sense. But that is what you're doing."

The witness of the Spirit says this, "God placed His laws in your heart when you became a Christian, He wrote them in your mind, and your sins and iniquities He remembers no more!" Get out of the flesh, walk in the Spirit, and let the Word of God come alive and be real in you. Listen, the Word of God and the carnal mind are at enmity with one another. Remember though, the Holy Ghost witnesses to the the Word of God inside you and not your carnal mind.

So then, my confession is, "I'm sanctified. I'm perfected. God doesn't remember my sins and failures, therefore I won't either."

This is powerful teaching for you. Jesus offered himself once! That was enough. The job is done. I'm sanctified, I'm perfected. I don't have to get there, I already am. I just am - the Word says that I am. "Well, Brother Jay, there are things in my life that are not quite right." Hang on, brother, God's not through with you yet. I can look back over my life as a Christian and see things that over the years God has purged out. I look at my life RIGHT NOW and see things that I don't like and don't want to be there. But I remind myself of Philippians 1:6,

How To Exercise God's Megaton Power Now

Phil. 1:6

6 Being confident of this very thing, that he which hath begun a good work in you will perform it until the day of Jesus Christ:

I have confidence that God will keep on working on me. If there are things in my life that shouldn't be, and I try the best I can to overcome it and fall short, I lie back and rest on the power of God to pick up my case and carry it on for me, knowing that He's working on me, He's still shaping me into the image of His dear Son. It's supernatural, it's grace, and God is NOT through with me. God speaks in a once for all fashion - and in His mind we ARE perfected - but if we're not there in our own mind, hang on, the ride's not over. This merry-go-round has another lap or two to run, and all the while God's on the hobby horse with us, working on us.

Examine your life over the past year. You are farther down the road spiritually now than you were then. Yet as we look at ourselves now, we feel that we're still not where we should be, but listen, we're farther than we were. If you'll walk close to God, he'll do the work for you and in you, and this time next year you'll look back and realize that you are farther down the spiritual road than you are today. Why? Because Philippians 1:6 is a spiritual truth we need to latch on to, and be confident in. It's ironic to me that Paul starts that verse to that little church in Philippi with the words, "Be confident." Be confident of this one thing. He which has begun a good work in you will keep on performing it until the day of Jesus Christ. Is that Scripture? Is it the truth? Is God working on us, or did He lie? Absolutely not!

Listen, God's going to do what He said whether you like it or even realize it. So, be confident. God's not through with you yet. In His mind, the job is finished - you're sanctified and perfected. But if in your mind there is a little left to do, don't worry, He'll get around to it. Be confident that He will. He will perform that good work in you. That word perform is in the Greek present tense, which means continuous action in present time. So, what that Scripture actually says that He will not only perform the good work but will keep on keeping on performing it until the day of Jesus Christ. You'll go deeper and deeper into the things of God. That's shouting ground!

One offering sanctified and perfected us forever. No wonder we can come boldly into the holiest (verse 19)! It's by the blood of Jesus. I have no hope apart from the blood of Jesus. I've staked my all on that blood. If that blood is a farce, of all men, I am the most in trouble, because I have cast everything on that blood. And that's where I rest my case.

When Jesus said, "Be ye therefore perfect as you father in heaven is perfect", he simply meant, "Be what you are as your father in heaven is being what he is". We are *perfect now*. We are complete. Peter knew this truth and acted upon it. You must *know* it also. Then you can act upon it also.

The Five Bedrock Foundations of Megaton Power and Why You Can Stand On Them Now

CHAPTER 7

The Shedding Of Jesus' Blood And What This Does To Power You Up Now

In this chapter I want to address what the shedding of Jesus' blood does to power you up today. To begin let's look at a portion of Hebrews chapter 9.

> Heb 9:19-26
> 19 For when Moses had spoken every precept to all the people according to the law, he took the blood of calves and of goats, with water, and scarlet wool, and hyssop, and sprinkled both the book, and all the people,
> 20 Saying, This is the blood of the testament which God hath enjoined unto you.
> 21 Moreover he sprinkled with blood both the tabernacle, and all the vessels of the ministry.
> 22 And almost all things are by the law purged with blood; and without shedding of blood is no remission.
> 23 It was therefore necessary that the patterns of things in the heavens should be purified with these; but the heavenly things themselves with better

> sacrifices than these.
> 24 For Christ is not entered into the holy places made with hands, which are the figures of the true; but into heaven itself, now to appear in the presence of God for us:
> 25 Nor yet that he should offer himself often, as the high priest entereth into the holy place every year with blood of others;
> 26 For then must he often have suffered since the foundation of the world: but now once in the end of the world hath he appeared to put away sin by the sacrifice of himself.

Verse 22 say apart from the shedding of blood, individuals had no way to get out from under the curse or the penalty of sin. Without the shedding of the blood of animals under the law there was no remission for the sins of the people.

In verse 23 substitute the word **copy** for the word **patterns** in this verse. That will help you to understand what the verse is saying more easily. What he is saying is that it was necessary that the copy of things in heaven should be purified with these, that is with the blood of bulls and goats.

When Moses built the tabernacle upon which was based the structure of the temple, God actually showed Moses the interior of heaven, and Moses was instructed to make a copy of what he saw in the form of a portable structure. That portable structure was called the tabernacle. It could be moved anywhere the Spirit led the children of Israel to move it. For the sake of simplicity I'm going to deal with just that part of the tabernacle that is divided into two parts.

The part we will talk about is called the Holy of Holies. It was into the Holy of Holies that the high priest went once each year on the Day of Atonement. Inside this structure Moses had set up in the same order the same things he saw in heaven - an alter, tables, instruments of various kinds, and candle sticks. He copied things at the express command of God. He made a portable copy of what he saw in heaven.

How To Exercise God's Megaton Power Now

The writer of the book of Hebrews said that it was necessary that these copies be purified with these, or the blood of animals. But he goes on to say that the heavenly things themselves had to be purified with better sacrifices than these. The blood of bulls and goats dealt with the sin problem on the earth, and they could sprinkle the copies of those instruments with the blood of bulls and goats. But it would have been a blaspheme to enter into heaven and sprinkle the blood of bulls and goats there. So he said that the things in heaven had to be purified with a better sacrifice - a more powerful, more potent, more eternal, more deified blood than the blood of bulls and goats.

Then he says

> Hebrews 9:24,
> 24   For Christ is not entered into the holy places made with hands, which are the figures of the true; but into heaven itself, now to appear in the presence of God for us:

Now notice, there is the Holy of Holies in heaven. Moses copied it and made it in the form of a portable tent. Later, what he saw and copied was turned into the pattern for the stationary temple in Jerusalem. But all of it was a copy of what Moses saw in heaven. There is the earthly Holy of Holies in the tabernacle and later in the temple, and there is also the one in heaven which Moses copied. The high priest on earth during that time would go into the earthly Holy of Holies once a year, and the blood that he would sprinkle would be good for the passing over of the sins of the people for a space of one year. Every April the Day of Atonement occurred, the earthly high priest would go into the portable tent, and later the temple, and he would sprinkle the interior of the Holy of Holies with the blood of bulls and goats. This sprinkling took care of the sins of those people for one full year.

Verse 24 says that Christ did not enter that earthly Holy of Holies. But it says that He entered into the holy place, or into heaven itself, to appear in the presence of God for us. The Jewish high priest would go into the earthly Holy of Holies and appear in the presence of God once a year. Christ never entered into that place a time in His life. Instead, He entered into that part of heaven from which that earthly copy was derived. And there he entered into the presence of God for us.

How To Exercise God's Megaton Power Now

> Hebrews 9:25-26
> 25 Nor yet that he should offer himself often, as the high priest entereth into the holy place every year with blood of others;
> 26 For then must he often have suffered since the foundation of the world: but now once in the end of the world hath he appeared to put away sin by the sacrifice of himself.

Those high priests in the Jewish religious system had to go into the earthly Holy of Holies once a year, and they always entered with the blood of others - bulls and goats, but not their own blood. Christ did not have to offer Himself often, He had to do it only one time. I want you to see the power, potency, and duration of the blood of Christ compared with the blood of an animal.

The blood of bulls and goats when used by the high priest going into the earthly Holy of Holies was good enough to care for the sin problem of an entire nation for twelve solid months. But every twelve months they had to repeat the process. This meant that every twelve months there was a slaughter of animals. Verse 24 says that Christ never entered that Holy of Holies but He entered the one in heaven. And notice in verse 25 that He did not have to offer Himself often. In other words, Christ had to be slain only one time for the sin problem. Since He had to be slain only one time His blood has the power to care for the sin problem for how long - for eternity.

What I want you to see is this. If, in fact, the power of the blood of Christ runs out in a given time span - if it runs out in less than a year, that means the blood of a bull and goat had more power to it in the mind of God than the blood of His own Son. I'm talking about the blood of Jesus compared to the blood of bulls and goats. The blood of these animals when handled properly in the Old Testament lasted a year. But the blood of Jesus Christ lasts beyond a year. Otherwise, once a year Jesus would have to come back down from heaven and be slain again. Then He would have had to suffer since the foundation of the world. But verse 26 says that once, or one time in the end of the world, he appeared to put away sin by the sacrifice of Himself.

How To Exercise God's Megaton Power Now

Are you aware of the fact that if a Jew sinned under the Old Testament law and he had participated in that national Day of Atonement that the sin that he committed was covered by the blood of that Atonement for a twelve month period. And yet a lot of Christians do great insult to the blood of Jesus because they maintain that if they sin they instantly lose whatever it was they had from God, that is, their salvation. They don't recognize the fact that this is an insult to the blood of Jesus Christ, because they are saying that the blood of Christ did not have the staying power of even the blood of a goat! That's an insult. What else could you call it, but an insult. Even the blood of a bull and goat lasted a year, and yet some people want to maintain the blood of Christ doesn't even last ten seconds. He appeared once, and He put away sin by the sacrifice of Himself. And that sacrifice does not need to be repeated every twelve months. It was a one time thing.

> Heb 9:27-28
> 27   And as it is appointed unto men once to die, but after this the judgment:
> 28   So Christ was once offered to bear the sins of many; and unto them that look for him shall he appear the second time without sin unto salvation.

Verse 27 is one of those verses which we often take out of context and preach evangelistic sermons. We can preach a practical evangelistic message with this passage, but let me show you how it fits contextually with what we are talking about. This verse is talking about Jesus Christ. God became a man. He took the Name of Jesus Christ when He walked on this earth. Since it is appointed unto man once to die, and Jesus became a man, He died. But He died in our place. He died my death. He died your death. He died because of my sins. He died because of your sins. After the appointment that man has with death there is also an appointment with judgment. Christ became a man, Christ died in my place, and Christ took the judgment for my sin.

How can God judge Jesus for my sin and still hold my sin against me? How can Jesus' blood be more powerful than the blood of bulls and goats if I can lose what I have in Christ in ten seconds. Even the Jew in the Old Covenant couldn't do that. The blood of those animals on the Day of Atonement covered their sin for the space of twelve long months. It was not necessary for the high priest to go into the Holy of Holies every twelve seconds or every twelve days. Can the blood of Christ last any less?

My hope is built on nothing less than Jesus' blood and righteousness! This is where we need to learn to stand, and when we learn to stand there we will have the key to reigning in life as kings. Until we understand the power in the blood of Jesus we will not reign with power.

Now let's look further at Hebrews chapter 10.

> Heb 10:1-4
> 1   For the law having a shadow of good things to come, and not the very image of the things, can never with those sacrifices which they offered year by year continually make the comers thereunto perfect.
> 2   For then would they not have ceased to be offered? because that the worshippers once purged should have had no more conscience of sins.
> 3   But in those sacrifices there is a remembrance again made of sins every year.
> 4   For it is not possible that the blood of bulls and of goats should take away sins.

The law that he is speaking of in verse 1, Moses' law of sacrificing once a year on the Day of Atonement, was never designed to make the people perfect. The word "perfect" is derived from a Greek word which means to come to the end of a process. The end of the process that was being spoken of in this case was a place in their lives where there would be no more necessity for more sacrifices for their sin. The law could never do that. For every year under Moses' law the high priest had to take the blood of others, go behind the veil that shut out the common man, and enter into the place where only he was authorized to go. Every year he had to do it, and he could never, never, never bring the people to a state of completion where, under the law, those sacrifices could be terminated. That process was never fulfilled under the law.

But Jesus Christ came and became the final sacrifice for sin under Moses' law. So what the law could not do, He did. The law could never, with those sacrifices which they offered year after year continually, make those who participated come to the end of the sacrificial process. That is what the word perfect in that context means.

Verse 2 is a key verse **IF** you want to have power for reigning in life as a king. It's an extremely important key verse! If, in fact, the act of slaughtering bulls and goats and the high priest going behind the veil in the earthly tabernacle, could have brought the people to the end of the process of needing sacrifices, then they would have ceased making sacrifices because once they made the sacrifices they would have had no more conscience of the guilt of their sins. Because the sacrificing would have done the job.

Let's compare that to the blood of Christ. First of all, look at Hebrews 10:3. Suppose someone had a full life; he lived in the fast food lane of life, so busy that all he had time to do was drive through the drive through lane and eat on the run. He was so busy that he never had time to think about his sins. But once a year he would have to think about them. Once a year he would participate in the Day of Atonement. Once a year he would go back to Jerusalem and would be absolved of his sins by the blood of bulls and goats. But each year at that time, no matter how busy he was, he would be reminded in his conscience, "I have a sin problem." The fact that it was yearly, year after year, reminded him of who he was, what he had done, and the consequences of it. Now, if the blood of bulls and goats had been the answer, he would not have had to be reminded once a year of who he was and what he had done, and what the logical outcome was of the fact that he had committed sins and he was a sinner.

This is to be contrasted with the blood of Jesus Christ which does not have to be shed every twelve months. This means that I can lose myself in doing God's business and living my life for Him. And I don't have to be reminded and have my conscience pricked, week in and week out, month in and month out, year in and year out about my sin problem because Jesus Christ was offered ONCE to take away sin. And His blood is more powerful than the blood of a bull or a goat.

How To Exercise God's Megaton Power Now

Therefore, since His blood is more powerful, and their blood lasted a full year, how long does the blood of Jesus Christ last? Now when you get a revelation of this, you can begin to get the Devil out of your face so that you have power to reign in life.

As long as the Devil backs you in a corner and makes you accept a lesser view of the blood of Christ and what that blood does, he will rob you of your power and you will never reign in life as a king. We read the books, we make the confessions, we talk the talk. But if we have a defective view of the blood of Christ, we will always be backed into a corner, and our reigning will go down the tube.

How long did the blood of Christ last? These scriptures say that He appeared once in the end of the age and He put away sin by the sacrifice of Himself - ONCE. There is no place in Scripture that puts a time limit on the efficacy, the power, and the cleansing ability of the blood of Jesus. NO WHERE! I challenge you to find it, but until you do, don't let the Devil deceive you by making you think less of the blood of Christ than what God says about it.

Once a year the Old Testament people were reminded that they had a sin problem, but if all the sacrificing that they were doing had worked, they would not have been reminded of it over and over again. Well, the blood of Jesus does work, so why should I be reminded EVER? I am free from that problem because the blood of Jesus Christ is strong enough to deal with it.

When someone challenges me on this, I know that I am talking to someone who believes that the blood of Jesus doesn't have the power that the blood of a bull or does has. How powerful **IS** the blood of Christ? What is it's duration? The power of the blood of bulls and goats lasted twelve months, but every twelve months the high priest had to kill more to get more blood because it ran out. But the Bible says that Jesus Christ was offered ONCE. Now if they did not have a conscience of their sin problem except once a year, why is it that we do? In Hebrews 10:4 it says,

Heb 10:4

4 For it is not possible that the blood of bulls and of goats should take away sins.

Look at the words "<u>not possible</u>." That means there is no power in the blood of a bull or a goat to take away sin. There is no capability in it. So all that happened is that the sin was just covered up for a year. But 1 John 1:7 says that the blood of His Son Jesus Christ cleanseth us. And in the Greek present tense that means continuous action in present time. It means that it cleanses and keeps on keeping on cleansing me from all sin; not for only twelve months, but a keeping on keeping on. It means you are in a continual wash cycle. Continually being washed by the blood of the Lamb. When you understand the "once for all sacrifice", when you understand that Christ's blood had more power than the blood of bulls and goats, you will begin to concentrate on what the Bible says belongs to you rather than letting the Devil back you in a corner over something you did or did not do. As long as the Devil has you on the defense you will never have power for reigning.

In the eighth chapter of the book of Romans Paul talked about us reigning in life as kings. But there are keys to that. One key is that we have to accept the free gift of being cleared of all the guilt of all our sins. Another key is that we have to accept the fact that Jesus Christ's blood has more duration, more power to it than the blood of bulls and goats which lasted twelve months. They had to be slaughtered every year, but Jesus was offered up at the end of this age **ONE TIME.**

What we fail to recognize is that if that one sacrifice of Jesus didn't work and Jesus is still claiming to be the Savior, then He has to move Himself out of heaven once a year, come back down here, and be nailed to the cross all over again and again and again - every time we commit a sin. If His blood didn't have power enough to cover the sin problem throughout all eternity, it would require Him to come back, die again, be resurrected again - come back, die again, be resurrected again - over and over again. That's the logical conclusion if His blood is not eternal and does not extend beyond the twelve month duration of the blood of bulls and goats.

How To Exercise God's Megaton Power Now

When you get a handle on this you will have power to look the Devil, the accuser of the brethren, right in the eyeballs and say, "Get out of my way, you dirty Devil!"

Jesus Christ died once, because that's all it took. And the blood that He shed is lasting until this hour. Many people think that when Jesus was crucified and His blood was shed that it just soaked into the ground and was washed away with the elements. But the Bible teaches in the book of Hebrews that Jesus took His blood into heaven, and it is now sprinkled on the mercy seat - the same mercy seat that Moses saw and built a copy of. That blood is on the original mercy seat of heaven right now - still alive, still powerful, still fresh, and still working. The only way that Jesus' blood would lose it's power is if someone could go into heaven with some powerhouse form of cleanser, pour it on top of the blood sprinkled over the mercy seat of heaven, and dilute it down to where it has less power than the blood of a bull or a goat. But until someone is capable of doing that, mark my word, the blood of Jesus Christ, His Son, **cleanseth us from all sin and keeps on keeping on cleansing us from all sin!**

There is one thing that I will not allow. I will not allow the Devil to dictate my theology. Stop letting the Devil tell you what the Bible says. You tell him what the Bible says. He tried doing that to Jesus in the wilderness, but Jesus turned it on him and said, "It is written......" And when the Devil comes after you with a guilt trip, you tell him about the blood of Jesus Christ. That is one weapon that he cannot tangle with and win. When he sees that you know what you're talking about, guess what he will do? He's going to flee! He'll be in the next county before you can bat your eyes. Because the blood of Jesus Christ, His Son, cleanseth and keeps on cleansing us from all sin. Hallelujah!

The Five Bedrock Foundations of Megaton Power And Why You Can Stand On Them Now

CHAPTER 8

The Three Sprinklings Of Jesus' Blood And What This Does To Power You Up Now

There are four things we must settle concerning the blood of Jesus before we can correctly appropriate it and power up with it. Number one - What is the great importance about the blood of Jesus? What makes His blood any different from anybody else's? Number two - What is the relationship of the blood of Jesus to the Abrahamic Covenant? Number three - What does the Bible mean when it talks about sprinkling of blood, and what is the differences between the sprinkling of the blood of Jesus versus the sprinkling of the blood of a bull or goat. Number four - How does this apply to us today.

A lot of the problems that Christians experience is a result of a defective view of the blood of Jesus. Once we have the proper concepts fixed firmly in our minds concerning His blood, we will find that our lives are going to be different.

Let's answer the first question. What is so special about the blood of Jesus? What's different about His blood? Why couldn't the blood of a Roman soldier accomplish the same thing that Jesus' blood did?

How To Exercise God's Megaton Power Now

Look at Acts 20:28.

> 28 Take heed therefore unto yourselves, and to all the flock, over the which the Holy Ghost hath made you overseers, to feed the church of God, which he hath purchased with his own blood.

Notice that the purchase price that is paid for the church is the blood of God. We all know that God is the Father, Jesus is the Son, and the Holy Ghost is the third member of the Godhead. We talk a lot about the blood of Jesus, and yet this verse says that the church was purchased with the blood of God. If, in fact, Jesus was the Son of God only, why does this Scripture say that the church was purchased with the blood of God? Why didn't it say purchased with the blood of the Son of God? Because Jesus was the Son of God for the simple reason that God created His body. But Jesus Christ was more than the Son of God, Jesus Christ WAS God. John 1:1 declares,

> John 1:1
> 1 In the beginning was the Word, and the Word was with God, and the Word was God.

And John 1:14 says that same Word was made flesh and dwelt among us. In other words, two thousand years ago God, the same God that spoke everything into being, the same God that holds everything in orbit in it's place by the power of His spoken Word, stepped out of eternity and entered time and became flesh. God was born and lived and walked on this earth, beginning as a little baby named Jesus and growing up into a man who died as God in a human body.

What is different about the blood of Jesus, and why is it so important? When Jesus came, Jesus was God, and the blood that was inside His body was God's own blood. It was energized by the power of God and the life that was in it was the life of God. Jesus had no male parent; therefore, the life that was in his flesh was in His blood. But the life that was in His blood was the life of eternity itself, for His blood was energized by God. That's the difference between the blood of Jesus and the blood of a Roman soldier or any other man. The blood of Jesus is important because literally it was the blood of God, and that blood purchased the church of God, whose church we are right now.

The second thing I want us to see is that the blood of Jesus is not just the blood of God but is something else also. Look at Hebrews 13:20.

> Heb 13:20
> 20 Now the God of peace, that brought again from the dead our Lord Jesus, that great shepherd of the sheep, through the blood of the everlasting covenant,

When God raised Jesus from the dead, He did it through the blood. And here He calls that blood the "the blood of the everlasting covenant". I want you to get this term fixed in your mind. I want to share with you exactly what it means, so that when you hear the expression "the blood of Jesus" it will set off bells and whistles in your spirit, because the blood of Jesus Christ will take on new meaning for you.

What does it mean God raised Jesus from the dead through the same blood which He calls the blood of the everlasting covenant? The everlasting covenant is no more or no less than the Abrahamic Covenant. Abraham was a man just like you and I. God singled him out by His grace and His sovereignty with the intention of doing things through him that He had never done before with the human race. God gave him things that were to belong to him and that he was to pass on to his children, whether those children were his physical descendants or spiritual descendants. He set up a covenant with Abraham that would be eternal. What God promised him would never pass away. The things that God would tell Abraham would last forever. This is the same covenant that God made with Jesus Christ, His Son, before the world was framed. He would begin now to work it out through time beginning with Abraham. What God promised Abraham would belong to all Christians and would last forever. And He then sealed the covenant with blood.

Now pay close attention to what I'm about to say. That Abrahamic Covenant appears in the book of Genesis, in chapters 12, 13, 15, 17, and 22. There are 60 different promises God made to Abraham, everyone of which is an eternal promise. All of these promises apply and belong to us because Christians are included in that series of 60 promises. So the covenant is an eternal promise for you and me, as it was for Abraham, Isaac, Jacob, and the children of Israel. God in essence said, "Abraham, I'm going to set into motion these promises. They're going to be eternal, they will last forever throughout eternity, and I'm going to seal it in blood."

How was all this going to take place though? There was in those days what was known as a blood covenant of friendship. Two people would enter into covenant and both would shed blood. They would seal the agreement in blood. They would do this with their own blood, or they would do it with the blood of a substitute, as in an animal sacrifice. Then they would have a feast, eating flesh and drinking blood; not usually their own, although savages did. In the Bible they would eat the flesh of an animal, but instead of drinking it's blood, they would drink wine or juice. (This is where our Lord's Supper originates from.)

Now the blood of the covenant is simply this. When God and Abraham made the covenant, Abraham had to shed his own blood through circumcision. God shed blood through a sacrificial animal (Genesis 15 and 17). Jesus ratified the Abrahamic Covenant when he ascended Golgatha to be nailed to the cross. His own blood flowed out of his body as it was cut to ribbons, His hands and feet were sliced open as he was nailed to the cross, and He was stabbed with a spear. At that point in time the blood of God Himself was shed completing the Abrahamic Covenant from the God-ward side. So the death of Christ simply ratified what God had promised Abraham would last forever.

Up to that time all male Jews had to be circumcised, but when Jesus came and the blood of God was shed, then circumcision stopped, because the covenant was completed. Now we have what is known as a completed covenant. God raised Jesus from the dead through the blood of that everlasting covenant which is the Abrahamic Covenant. So then, it is the blood of God Himself that 1) bought the Church and 2) enabled Jesus Christ to be raised from the dead through it, because it was the blood of God's own body that was shed for the ratification of the Abrahamic Covenant.

Understand though, that this covenant was not complete until Jesus came and completed it. He ratified Abraham's Covenant. So, the blood of Jesus Christ is 1) the blood of God, and 2) the blood of the everlasting covenant which Jesus ratified sealing for us the promise of salvation, healing, and prosperity.

Let's look at the third point - the sprinkling of blood. How does the blood of Jesus affect us? Since it is the blood of God and the blood of the everlasting covenant, how do we apply it and make it real in our own lives? You see, we plead the blood, but we don't have the slightest idea what we're doing. We don't know how it works. We don't know what it is. We know that it's the blood of Jesus, but we don't know what the ramifications of His blood are. What does the blood of Jesus have to do with me? And how does God deal with me because of the blood? We have to go back and get some Old Testament background information on the law which God set up under Moses. We find that information in Hebrews 9:19-22.

> Heb 9:19-22
> 19   For when Moses had spoken every precept to all the people according to the law, he took the blood of calves and of goats, with water, and scarlet wool, and hyssop, and sprinkled both the book, and all the people,
> 20   Saying, This is the blood of the testament which God hath enjoined unto you.
> 21   Moreover he sprinkled with blood both the tabernacle, and all the vessels of the ministry.
> 22   And almost all things are by the law purged with blood; and without shedding of blood is no remission.

The word "testament" in verse 20 is the Greek word DIATHAKA, which means "covenant". When you see the word testament, to make it more understandable, translate it covenant. Now look at the word "purged" in verse 22. It comes from the Greek word KATHARIDZO, which means to "cleanse or purify". We get our word catheter from this Greek word.

How To Exercise God's Megaton Power Now

We understand that the blood of Jesus Christ is the blood of God, the blood of the eternal covenant, but how is it applied? According to the Old Testament law, everything had to be cleansed by blood. How was it done? By being dunked or baptized? No, by being sprinkled. So to cleanse something you sprinkled blood on it. Moses sprinkled the book and the people, the tabernacle and the vessels inside it, and verse 22 says that almost all things are by the law cleansed or purged by the sprinkling of blood. In the Old Testament the blood of bulls and goats was used, but that has passed away. Now there is the THREE SPRINKLINGS of another blood, THE BLOOD OF JESUS.

> Heb 9:13-14
> 13 For if the blood of bulls and of goats, and the ashes of an heifer sprinkling the unclean, sanctifieth to the purifying of the flesh:
> 14 How much more shall the blood of Christ, who through the eternal Spirit offered himself without spot to God, purge your conscience from dead works to serve the living God?

Do you see the relationship between the sprinkling of the blood of bulls and goats and the sprinkling of the blood Jesus?

Remember now, Jesus' blood is the blood of God. As such, it was the blood poured out to fulfill the Abrahamic Covenant. And now that blood, like the blood of bulls and goats in the Old Testament, must be sprinkled. But there is a difference in the sprinkling of the blood of Jesus and the blood of bulls and goats. When they sprinkled the blood of bulls and goats, they had to do it over and over and over and over. But when the blood of Jesus was spilled, since it is an eternal blood, then that sprinkling is an eternal sprinkling. It only has to be done once.

I want to make sure that you see and understand the sprinkling of blood. Moses sprinkled the book, he sprinkled the people, he sprinkled the tabernacle, he sprinkled the vessels of the ministry, he sprinkled almost all things in order to make them clean.

Brother Jay, what does all this have to do with me? It's the sprinkling of the blood in the salvation process that gets you saved. We all know that we're redeemed by the blood of Jesus. We all know that Jesus is the satisfaction for the sins of the world through faith in His blood. But how do we have faith in His blood? When someone tells me to have faith in something, what are they talking about?

If I had died before I was 23 years old, I would have gone to hell. Do you know why? Nobody could explain to me what they meant when they said, "Believe on the Lord Jesus Christ." They kept telling me, "Have faith." But I didn't know what they meant. I had two Sunday School teachers when I was in high school who would witness to me all the time, because they wanted to get me saved. I'll never forget what they did, and I appreciate it to this day. I had a Godly pastor who talked to me about being saved. My parents prayed for me and talked to me about it. But I was hung up on one concept. I did not know what they meant when they said, "Believe." I didn't know what they meant when they used the word "Faith". I believed that Jesus was who He said He was, but I said, "I don't feel saved." I just couldn't get a handle on "Faith". Now, my whole ministry is built around showing people what faith is and helping to stabilize and make them solid. I'm not interested in making people into a bunch of sky rocket Christians. I want you to know who you are, what you have, where you came from, where you're going, and how you're going to get there. I know what faith is now, because the Holy Ghost finally taught it to me. Faith is knowing the will of God in advance and then acting on it. For when you know the will of God, that knowledge is your faith. And when you believe, you'll act on that knowledge.

So when the Bible says that we are to have faith in the blood of Jesus, that means that I've got to know some things about it. I've got to know what's different about it. I have to know that the blood of Jesus Christ is the blood of God Himself in human form. I have to know that Jesus' blood was the very blood that ratified the everlasting covenant between God and Abraham. I have to KNOW it. And when Jesus shed His blood, it was God saying in essence, "Now I've put My own stamp of approval on the Abrahamic Covenant. Everything in it is now yours, because I ratified it with My own blood." The blood of Jesus Christ is something solid upon which you can stand and base your hope.

I have to know that in the Old Testament they cleaned things by sprinkling the blood of bulls and goats on it. And I have to know that the same concept is followed in the New Testament, except not with the blood of bulls and goats, but with the blood of Jesus.

> 1 Pet 1:2
> 2 Elect according to the foreknowledge of God the Father, through sanctification of the Spirit, unto obedience and sprinkling of the blood of Jesus Christ: Grace unto you, and peace, be multiplied.

So people are elect according to the foreknowledge of God the Father through two things. Do you want to know what it means to be an elect of God? There are two things that makes it happen through the foreknowledge of God: sanctification of the Spirit, and sprinkling of the blood of Jesus Christ. When someone receives Jesus Christ as their personal Savior, two things happen simultaneously. Number one, the blood of Jesus Christ is sprinkled over that person by the Holy Ghost. And second, the Holy Ghost separates that person from then on for the use of God. (Sanctify means to separate.) You don't have anything to do with it, God does it. When you receive Jesus as your personal Savior, all your old past sins come under the sprinkling of the blood of Jesus, and the moment you are sprinkled all the past is gone and you stand clean before Almighty God.

Go back to Hebrews 9:22 again. "And almost all things are by the law purged with blood...." Again, the word purged is the Greek word KATHARIDZO, from which comes our word catheter - a means to cleanse the inner body. And the blood sprinkled is God's cleansing agent. Brother and sister, that eliminates any hope for works - me doing this or that. It's the sprinkling of the blood of Jesus that does the cleansing, or YOU'RE NOT CLEAN! It's as simple as that. The moment you are sprinkled with that precious blood of Jesus, bless God, you ARE the elect.

So, the blood of Jesus is the entrance into the door of salvation. And just like all things are by the law cleansed by the sprinkling of blood, the moment you receive Jesus as your Savior you are sprinkled by God Himself with the blood of God Himself. You become clean on the one hand, and separated on the other. It's a supernatural act; you have nothing to do with it, except receive what God has done.

How To Exercise God's Megaton Power Now

We're sprinkled in order to get us clean for salvation, but there are two other sprinklings that happen to us once we are saved. Each person undergoes THREE SPRINKLINGS of the blood of God, the blood of the everlasting covenant. The first SPRINKLING brings us into the elect, but the other two make changes after the cleansing has occurred.

> Heb 10:22
> 22 Let us draw near with a true heart in full assurance of faith, having our hearts sprinkled from an evil conscience, and our bodies washed with pure water.

What does this mean, "..having our hearts sprinkled from an evil conscience.."? I'll illustrate the meaning like this. If I said that "Joe had an injury from an auto accident," I would simply mean that the auto accident caused his injury. Consequently, the verse above says that our hearts need cleansing because our conscience, our voice of our spirit man, has been evil. In other words, our evil conscience has left our heart in need of cleansing. So the SECOND SPRINKLING of Jesus' blood, then, is our heart or our spirit man.

Let me explain something to you. The conscience is the voice of your spirit man. Every one has a spirit man. When you're lost your spirit man is in tune with the Devil. You can do things and your conscience won't bother you. But when you get saved your spirit changes, it's different. It now has the life of God in it. It has been sprinkled with the SECOND SPRINKLING OF JESUS' BLOOD. The Holy Ghost begins to speak the words of God into you, and when you do something that is a sin you automatically know it. You can feel it, and your conscience starts screaming at you.

When we are lost our conscience is an evil conscience. It will permit evil and will not say anything against evil. So when we get saved God has to do a number on that evil conscience. He has to change it so that it is able to tell you when you're doing something that is not right, because when you're lost your conscience simply doesn't operate like that. Now your conscience can pick up words of fear from your parents. For instance, my Mother used to say, "If you do that I'm going to tear you up!" And when I did it, my conscience warned me - it didn't bother me that what I had done was wrong. What bothered me was that I was going to get my seat blistered. So my conscience warned me of that kind of thing. But I didn't give any thought to the concept that I had wronged God. That didn't bother me much, because my conscience was evil, as was the rest of me.

So, there has to be something happen to clean up the evil conscience so that it no longer functions like that. What is it? "Our hearts are sprinkled from an evil conscience." There is a sprinkling of the blood of Jesus directly to our heart which changes the voice of the spirit, which is our conscience, so that we can draw near with a true heart in full assurance of faith.

I see Christians belaboring the fact of their sins, and this bothers me. It tells me that you have not yet mastered the doctrine of THE THREE SPRINKINGS OF THE BLOOD OF JESUS. You still have a defective view of the blood of Jesus Christ, because once you understand the work of the blood as it is sprinkled to your heart to get rid of your evil conscience, you will begin to stop thinking about your sin and start thinking more about the blood. The sprinkling that first cleansed you from sin is the same sprinkling that keeps on cleansing you from all sin. Remember 1 John 1:7, "...the blood of Jesus Christ his Son cleanseth us from all sin." This verse was written to Christians. Once you understand the function of the blood of Jesus your conscience will not register every little thing that happens. You'll shove it where it belongs - under the blood of Christ.

Why do I believe and teach so strong about the blood of Jesus? Because God wants us to walk in power; He wants us to reign in life as kings. But in order to reign, we are going to have to get rid of some ideas and beliefs which are weighing us down, because the power of God will never manifest itself where the people of God are so burdened down and under so much bondage because of past mistakes and sins which they think are so terrible. If that's all we think about we will never release the power of God out of our spirits.

So what we have to do is package up this sin problem and get it under the blood. For once it's under the blood we quit worrying about it. We go on with God and start manifesting the power of God. There will be no power of God as long as we are on a guilt trip, because we're not concentrating on releasing the power. In the back of our minds we're thinking, "I'm such a bad person; I'm not worthy for God to manifest Himself through me." You're right, you're not. But that has nothing to do with it. It's the blood of Christ that makes the difference. We must understand how the sprinkling of the blood of Jesus works.

Now let's look again at Hebrews 9:13-14 to see the THIRD SPRINKLING which Christians undergo.

> Heb 9:13-14
> 13   For if the blood of bulls and of goats, and the ashes of an heifer sprinkling the unclean, sanctifieth to the purifying of the flesh:
> 14   How much more shall the blood of Christ, who through the eternal Spirit offered himself without spot to God, purge your conscience from dead works to serve the living God?

Here is another reference to the conscience. First of all, the heart is sprinkled to get rid of the evil conscience. When this has occurred, there is still one problem that has to be dealt with. You see, the conscience is evil on one hand, and it's dirty on the other because of dead works. The conscience has a two-fold problem, both of which are dealt with by the sprinkling of the blood of Jesus. This is where most of us live - hung up because of our conscience. The spirit of man has to be sprinkled with blood because his conscience is evil. Once that evil has been removed from the heart by cleaning up his spirit, his conscience still has a problem because of dead works that he has been involved with.

Most people in the Christian realm, and this includes full-gospel people, are very religious. But all religious works are dead works. There is not one thing about a religious activity that is pleasing to God. The thing that pleases God is when the Spirit of God can manifest Himself spontaneously through Christians. Now there are some works which are pleasing to God. When you lay hands on the sick, that pleases God. When you go visit the fatherless and the widows, that pleases God. When you tithe and then give offerings, that pleases God. So there are some things which you can do, works which are not dead, that are pleasing to God. But there are a whole lot of things which we do that are dead works. This messes up the conscience, because the conscience has been lulled into sleep by thinking that all the things we do makes us religious. And God hates religion. I'm not a religious person - I'm a saved person with the Spirit of God living in me, and as I walk through life God lives through me. But I'm definitely not religious, in fact I refuse to be religious.

There are people whose "calling" is to go into churches and ministries and play church policeman. They want to tell pastors and ministers what they need to do and what not to do, when to do it and when not to do it. But let me tell you something; I've never had even one of those "policemen" go out into a parking lot with me to hand out gospel tracts. They think they're really religious. They're right, they are religious, but that's all they are. They are of no benefit to the Kingdom of God.

Now listen to me, until you understand that your conscience has been sprinkled, purged and cleansed, from dead works, it will be very hard for you to hear the Holy Ghost. The reason for that is your conscience has been buffeted to the place where it can't even sense the Spirit of God because your conscience is cluttered up with dead works. What we need to do is back off and subject everything we do to the sprinkling of the blood. For when the blood of Christ is applied to the work that we do for God's Kingdom, and is sprinkled on our conscience, then our conscience will filter out what shouldn't be there.

So, there are three sprinklings of the blood of Jesus which we must undergo. The first is the initial sprinkling where we are ushered into the body of the elect. When we receive Jesus as our Savior, simultaneously the Holy Ghost sanctifies us.

Let's stop right here and kick another religious work in the head. I've heard some of the weirdest sermons about what sanctification is since I've been in the full-gospel ranks, and it absolutely staggers my mind. Let me tell you what the word sanctify really means in the Greek New Testament. It has only one meaning; it means separated for somebody's use. When it says in 1 Peter 1:2 that we are elect through sanctification of the Spirit, that means the Spirit separated us the moment we received Christ Jesus as our Savior. We had absolutely nothing to do with it. God did it all. If we're separated at all, it's because of an act of the Holy Ghost, the grace of God, and the blood of Jesus. **MY HOPE IS BUILT ON NOTHING LESS THAN JESUS' BLOOD AND RIGHTEOUSNESS!!**

The second sprinkling is when the heart is cleansed by the blood of Jesus. The third sprinkling is when the conscience is purged because it is insensitive to the things of God - it's completely covered up with dead works of religion. Jesus said in John 14:12,

> John 14:12
> 12   Verily, verily, I say unto you, He that believeth on me, the works that I do shall he do also; and greater works than these shall he do; because I go unto my Father.

What did Jesus do? He laid His hands on sick people, and they got well. He cast devils out of people with His word. We can do that. Why? Because He said we could do it. And when our conscience has been subjected to the sprinkling of His blood, it becomes sensitive to the Holy Ghost, it can pick up and hear the voice of God. The conscience then turns around and talks to us. It says, "You can do whatever the Word of God says you can do!" Just do it!

These very things, THE THREE SPRINKLINGS, are what powered Peter up to heal the man at the gate Beautiful. They belong to you too. Never let the Devil rob you of your power by getting you on his proverbial "GUILT TRIP".

People Across The Country Are Saying:

The Most Life Changing Thing Ever Written On Healing And Prosperity Are The Author's Four Books On The Abrahamic Covenant:

- **What Are Abraham's Blessings Anyway?**
This Volume Explains Why Jesus *MUST H*eal and Prosper You Now.
- **What've They Done With Abraham's Blessings?**
This Volume Destroys The Modernistic Denial That Healing and Prosperity Belong To Christians Now
- **The Unbroken Force of Abraham's Blessings**
The Main Reason To Deny That Healing and Prosperity Belong To Christians Now, Defined, Examined, Refuted and Destroyed
- **How To Obtain Abraham's Blessings**
A Simple, Step by Step Guide To Obtaining The Healing, Prosperity and Well-being For Every Member of Your Family That God Promised You in The Abrahamic Covenant.

These Four Books Will Build Your Faith To A Fever Pitch. Order Yours Now, Here, Today. You'll Be Glad You Did!

The Five Bedrock Foundations of Megaton Power And Why You Can Stand On Them Now

CHAPTER 9

Your Conscience Sprinkled With Jesus' Blood And What This Does To Power You Up Now

In order to have power for reigning, there is one basic element that has to be dwelt with, and that's your conscience. It has to be dwelt with by and through the Blood of Jesus. As long as the Devil can trap you into having a bad conscience, you will have no power.

There are several things that you need to understand in order for your conscience to be straightened out. You have to have the proper understanding of the blood of Christ. You have to have the proper understanding of the high priestly ministry of Christ in heaven. You have to have the proper understanding of what Biblical righteousness is. You have to understand that righteousness is a free gift to us. You also have to understand the scheme of the Abrahamic Covenant and the relationship of Moses' law to it. Then you have to understand your own relationship to that covenant and to Moses' law. Until these things are worked out and settled in your mind, the Devil will quote you Scripture out of context, and he'll do a number on your conscience with misquoted Scripture. Until you surmount these obstacles and hurdles in your understanding, you will forever be on the defense. A person who is reeling from a punch, a person who has taken one on the jaw and is defensive, he's seeing stars because he's just been slammed with a giant fist of guilt is not a person who has power.

In order for us to have power we have to be on the offense. The only way we can do that is to know who we are by understanding these basic things that I just outlined. Then, and only then, will we have the power to reign in life - the power that Paul wrote about in the fifth chapter of the book of Romans.

> Rom 5:17
> 17 For if by one man's offence death reigned by one; much more they which receive abundance of grace and of the gift of righteousness shall reign in life by one, Jesus Christ.)

Now look at the word **conscience** in the following four verses in Hebrews:

> Heb 9:9
> 9 Which was a figure for the time then present, in which were offered both gifts and sacrifices, that could not make him that did the service perfect, as pertaining to the **conscience**;

> Heb 9:14
> 14 How much more shall the blood of Christ, who through the eternal Spirit offered himself without spot to God, purge your **conscience** from dead works to serve the living God?

> Heb 10:2
> 2 For then would they not have ceased to be offered? because that the worshippers once purged should have had no more **conscience** of sins.

> Heb 10:22
> 22 Let us draw near with a true heart in full

assurance of faith, having our hearts sprinkled from an evil **conscience**, and our bodies washed with pure water.

We find the same word, **conscience** or **consciousness** of sin. The writer of the book of Hebrews recognized a conscience problem, and he set himself to deal with it. I need to clarify something at this point. There is a difference between a Christian being conscious of the fact that he has done something he shouldn't have done (sinned), and his being conscious of the fact that that sin has been dealt with. Now for me to say that God has set up a mechanism whereby Christians can sin and not be conscious that they have sinned is wrong. Anybody who preaches that is wrong. But God has set up a mechanism, through the things which I have already mentioned to you at the beginning of this chapter, whereby we can recognize in our consciousness that our sin has been dealt with so that we are no longer accountable for it as far as judgment and eternal damnation is concerned. Do you understand the distinction? You must understand the difference, otherwise you will misread what I am about to teach you. There is a difference between a Christian being conscious of the fact that he has sinned, and being conscious of the fact that that sin has been dealt with by the blood of Christ.

We all have a conscience. The Devil plays with it and quotes Scripture to it. What we need to learn is the set of four Scriptures previously mentioned so we can quote them back to him. When he says to us, "Look at you; you sinned," we can reply, "Yes, but look at the blood of Jesus which dealt with it."

The conscience has a double role. Number one, it lets us know when we are walking outside the will of God; and number two, when we are in that state, it protects us from the Devil being able to quote us Scripture in order to keep us off course, by making us defensive, and losing our power. We have to maintain the ability for our conscience to point away from what we did to the blood of Christ as being that which deals with it. It always has to point to the priestly ministry of Christ. For right now, Jesus is not floating around heaven, He's very busy. He's our high priest, and when a Christian sins, according to 1 John 1:9, Jesus intercepts that sin and deals with it by pointing the face of God toward His blood sprinkled on the mercy seat. Jesus says, in so many words, "My blood is dealing with that sin now." Until these things are understood, you can sing the songs and talk the talk all day long about reigning as kings in life, but it will never happen because the Devil has you on the defense. Once you learn the things I'm teaching, you can go on the offense like Jesus did in the wilderness when the Devil quoted Him Scriptures out of context. Jesus took the Scripture and drove the Devil out of His presence, because Jesus knew who He was and where He stood with God. He literally beat the Devil over the head with the same Scripture that he quoted to Him. You can too when you learn what you're doing.

I'm the last guy in the world who can claim to be everything that I'm supposed to be, but there is one thing that I am, because I've made it my business to be. I do not let the Devil back me in a corner on a guilt trip, because I know the power of the blood of Jesus. I will not let him mess with me concerning the priestly ministry of Christ, the blood of Christ, or my relationship to the Abrahamic Covenant.

Now read Hebrews 9:7-12,

> Heb 9:7-12
> 7   But into the second went the high priest alone once every year, not without blood, which he offered for himself, and for the errors of the people:
> 8   The Holy Ghost this signifying, that the way into the holiest of all was not yet made manifest, while as the first tabernacle was yet standing:
> 9   Which was a figure for the time then present, in which were offered both gifts and sacrifices, that could not make him that did the service perfect, as pertaining to the conscience;
> 10   Which stood only in meats and drinks, and divers washings, and carnal ordinances, imposed on them until the time of reformation.
> 11   But Christ being come an high priest of good things to come, by a greater and more perfect tabernacle, not made with hands, that is to say, not of this building;
> 12   Neither by the blood of goats and calves, but by

his own blood he entered in once into the holy place, having obtained eternal redemption for us.

Notice that the high priest went into the Holy of Holies alone. The Jewish high priest had to make atonement for his own sins as well as the sins of the people. Jesus, our high priest, never had to make atonement for His sins, because He was sinless. But this high priest went in once a year with the blood of others and offered sacrifices for himself and the people.

Look at verse 8. The holiest of all is the Holy of Holies in heaven, and the way into the heavenly Holy of Holies was not yet prepared. You couldn't get into it yet because the first tabernacle on earth was still standing. Keep in mind that the tabernacle and later the temple, were copies of what Moses was allowed to see in heaven. God showed it to him, told him to copy it, and build it.

Verse 9 says that those sacrifices made by the Jewish high priest could not make the people perfect in the area of their conscience, because every year when the priest had to go back into the Holy of Holies on the Day of Atonement, they remembered again that there was no permanent answer for their sins. So their conscience was quickened again to the fact they were condemned because there was no remedy for their sins. Their conscience was their problem, and rightfully so because the blood of bulls and goats could not deal with the sin problem. It caused God to defer judgment, but it could not get rid of it. Once a year their conscience was reminded, "I am a sinner, I stand condemned, and there is no answer for my sin." The blood of animals just stalled judgment on it. It's the same as a man who is condemned and on death row, and he keeps getting one stay of execution after the other. This is what the Old Testament system of sacrifice did.

The Devil will do everything in his power to back you into that same corner, and if he can do it, you will have the same mind-set that the Old Testament people had. There will be no power in your life, because you will constantly be condemning yourself and making yourself fit into a sacrificial system that you were never under. The Devil works in the conscience and says, "Look what you did!" And you will say in return, "You're right, I did it," as though the blood of Christ didn't have the power that the blood of a bull or a goat did.

How To Exercise God's Megaton Power Now

Verse 11 states that Christ came to be a high priest of the original tabernacle that Moses saw in heaven; greater, more perfect, not made with human hands.

Now I want you to look at the word eternal in verse 12. Christ's own blood obtained a redemption that was an eternal redemption. He entered in once into the holy place. Keep in mind that the tabernacle and later the temple was built in two parts. There was the main part, then built onto the end of that was a smaller part. The people were separated from the smaller part by a veil. Behind the veil was the Holy of Holies.

But Jesus was not the high priest in this earthly Holy of Holies. When He died the veil that separated the people from that which was behind the veil was ripped in two, signifying that the way into the actual Holy of Holies in heaven was now open. Through Christ's death and the shedding of His blood, He entered the Holy of Holies in heaven one time. He went not with the blood others, but with His own blood, and He sprinkled the originals with His blood like the earthly priests did the copies down here with the blood of bulls and goats.

The blood of bulls and goats sprinkled in the earthly Holy of Holies lasted a year. It cared for the sins of the people for a solid year. The blood of Jesus sprinkled in the heavenly Holy of Holies lasts throughout eternity. The earthly high priest, who had to have blood shed for his own sins before he could sprinkle the blood for the sins of the people, went into the earthly Holy of Holies with the blood of animals, and that took care of the sins of an entire nation for a year.

But the Devil will try to make you think that the moment you sin, all is lost. What he is saying and trying to make you believe is that the blood of a bull, sprinkled by an earthly priest with sin problems himself, lasted a year, but the sinless priest and the blood of God Himself is not even good for 30 seconds. This makes absolutely no sense.

If you let the Devil rob you of your power because of sin problems, then you are a person who has never come to grips with the efficacy of the blood of Jesus Christ. The problem is that you have listened to the

How To Exercise God's Megaton Power Now

Devil tell you how sorry the blood of Christ really is. You need to get yourself anchored to the blood of Jesus, because once you are you won't be moved off every time you stumble. Listen, the Devil is always going to remind you of what you did.

But I don't need him to remind me of what I did - my conscience is already in tune with God. I know what I did! But, thank God, my conscience also reminds me that Christ's blood has already dealt with it. Most of us don't develop our theological base large enough and broad enough to have an effect on our conscience in that area. The Devil triggers your conscience every time you sin, but you don't know enough Scripture or if you do, you don't trust it enough to know in your conscience that that sin has been dealt with by the blood of Christ.

We must understand and accept the Biblical concept of righteousness. It means "clearance of all guilt". You've got to understand the power and the duration and the cleansing ability of the blood of Jesus Christ. You've got to understand the priestly ministry of Jesus Christ. You've got to understand your relationship with the Abrahamic Covenant. You've got to understand the relationship of Moses' law to that Covenant so when the Devil tells you that you're no good, you'll know how to put all this together in order to rightly divide the Word of truth. A Christian who has never paid the price in time to study and get grounded in the Word of God will be swept away into believing that there is no reason to even try to be good, because he seems to keep falling short of the glory of God. They'll throw up their hands and say, "Woe is me. The Devil is right. I can't measure up." When in fact, they do measure up.

There are too many Christians who are more interested in going to big "hip-hip-hoorah" conferences and meetings (not that there is anything wrong with it) than getting involved in and committed to a solid, Bible-teaching church where they can get the Word preached in depth so that they stand on their own feet and take up their place in the battle lines. This needs to change, Church. You may talk the talk, but you will never walk the walk until you grasp these basic principles I've talked about in this chapter and make them your very life. Most Christians try to establish their own righteousness, not realizing that righteousness is a free gift that they have to actively accept. Don't let the Devil or anyone else blow you out of the water concerning the fact that you are free of all guilt! Power is based on knowing certain things. You have power, but to appropriate that power you must know these Biblical concepts that I have outlined to you.

Power for reigning - the power is ours. We just don't walk in it because we've been convinced by the Devil that because of something we did or didn't do we've lost it. NO, you have not lost it. I pray for you, that you will understand the fullness of the finished work of Jesus Christ.

To sum up, the blood of Jesus cleanses our conscience from dead works. In the last chapter, we viewed those dead works as religious works. But they can also be just plain sin works. No matter. The blood of Jesus continuously cleanses us Christians from our sins. It also continually cleanses our conscience. So be bold and obtain.

The Five Bedrock Foundations of Megaton Power And Why You Can Stand On Them Now

CHAPTER 10

The High Priesthood Of Jesus And How It Functions To Power You Up Now

We need to define the function and purpose of a high priest. The high priest was the person in the Old Testament era who went before God on behalf of the people, because their ability to approach God was limited.

> Heb 4:14
> 14   Seeing then that we have a great high priest, that is passed into the heavens, Jesus the Son of God, let us hold fast our profession.

The writer of the book of Hebrews is showing that we Christians have a high priest who is not in the Holy of Holies on earth, but He's in the Holy of Holies in heaven. Jesus, the Son of God, is our high priest. He has passed from this world into the world to come.

What exactly is He doing there. Many people feel that since Jesus died and went back to heaven He's just sitting back in his recliner being a little lazy; that He has nothing to do except float around on the clouds, sail around Heaven, and sip a cold lemonade in His spare time.

How To Exercise God's Megaton Power Now

However, Jesus is functioning right now in a full-time job on our behalf. His function there is that of high priest. As high priest He goes before God every moment that the clock ticks on our behalf.

In the Old Testament people would bring their requests and needs to the high priest. He was an intermediary between what they said they needed and God. He would take their requests and then repeat them to God.

Jesus is in heaven right now as our high priest. In this capacity He is doing two things. Number one, He is taking care of our sin problem as Christians. His blood is continuously cleansing us of our sin. Part of Jesus' priestly office is the office of advocate. The devil still has access to heaven, and he is accusing us before God every time we sin. Our Advocate goes before God, like a lawyer before the judgment bar, and argues our case before Him. He points God's face away from our sin to His own blood, which is sprinkled on the mercy seat in heaven. That blood is still alive and fresh, and is as powerful today as it ever was. Jesus looks at His Father God and says, "My blood has canceled the sin that they did." Number two, Jesus, as our high priest, intercepts the prayers that we pray. He then goes before God the Father as our high priest, and He relays those prayers by repeating to the Father what we say. Jesus doesn't have time to float around Heaven all day doing nothing. He has a full time job.

The word translated "profession" in this verse, should have been translated with the English word "confession". The word confession in the Greek language combines two words - the word for "same" combined with the word "to say". So, confession or profession means to say the same thing. Our prayers are effective when we pray the same thing that God says in His Word. For when we say the same thing to a circumstance or in prayer that God says in His Word, those words are what Jesus intercepts as our high priest and goes before God with. This is how we get our prayers answered. Now if we pray something off the wall the high priest won't intercept it, but when we are saying the same thing, professing and confessing in our prayer the same God has already said in His Word, Jesus takes the prayer and relays it to God.

Therefore, the writer of the book of Hebrews said to that group of Hebrew Christians, "Let us hold fast saying the same thing with our lips that God said in His Word." Then he goes on to say some other things about Jesus in the next verse.

> Heb 4:15
> 15 For we have not an high priest which cannot be touched with the feeling of our infirmities; but was in all points tempted like as we are, yet without sin.

The average person views God as detached, distant, an impersonal force. They do not view God as a human being, but Jesus Christ was God in human flesh. The most staggering thing you can occupy your mind with is this - two thousand years ago God became a human being and walked this earth for thirty-three years. The name He took while He was here was the name Jesus. Jesus is God in human flesh. As such, He experienced every form of weakness and heartache that you will ever know. He understands you because He's been where you are. He knows what it's like to have a friend turn on Him and sell Him out. He knows what it's like to stand by the graveside of a loved one and weep. Jesus wept at the tomb of Lazarus. He knows where you are. He has felt what you feel. He knows loneliness. He knows, because He's been there. This verse says that we have not a high priest who cannot be touched with the feeling of our infirmities. This word infirmities is a word which means "absence of strength" or "weakness". He knows what it's like to be weak. He knows what poverty feels like. He's known heartache. He knows what it feels like to be deserted by friends. He walked the road before us. Therefore, when we go to Him as our great high priest He can identify with us by personal experience.

I used to think that God could care less about me. He didn't understand what I was feeling. He didn't understand how I was hurting. He didn't understand how I felt when people turned on me - they patted me on the back with one hand while the other hand had a knife in it ramming it in my back. I didn't think God understood anything I was going through. But He did, and He still does. We have not a high priest who cannot be touched with the feeling of our infirmities, because He was touched with same the feeling of infirmity.

How To Exercise God's Megaton Power Now

This verse tells me that I have the ear of God when I go before Him with a need or a hurt. He's already experienced everything we are going through. He's been hungry and needed food and water. He needed sleep. He needed fellowship. He needed companionship. He needed everything that you and I have ever needed. He's been there. Jesus Christ experienced even more than we have, because His sensitivities were very likely much deeper than ours. Therefore, He CAN be touched with our weaknesses. He may never have driven a car that won't start, but He knows the feeling. Because what He missed in that one experience, He picked up in another.

Thomas Jefferson, as brilliant as the man was, believed that God created the universe, wound it up like a clock, and set it on a shelf. And now He's keeping His hands off and letting the "clock" that He built tick, but He's not intervening in any of it's affairs. That is dead wrong. Thank God, we have a high priest who not only feels what we feel, but He cares. How can Thomas Jefferson be right when the Apostle Peter said in I Peter 5:7, "Casting all your care upon him; for he careth for you."

You can't convince me that somebody cares for me if they see me about to walk over the edge of a cliff, and they do nothing about it! If God backed off and let my "clock" run and did not interfere in my life and circumstances when He sees that I'm hurting and about to be destroyed, there would be no way for me to accept the fact that He gave a rip about me or anybody else.

Mr. Jefferson's belief is foolishness. We have not an high priest which cannot be touched with the feeling of our infirmities. This verse goes on to say that He was tempted in all points like as we are, yet without sin. The word tempted can mean "solicitation to sin" or it can mean "trial and tribulation". Chances are that in this passage it means trial and tribulation. He was in all points badgered and bombed and kicked and betrayed. He experienced tribulation, heartache, and grief, yet through it all He never resorted to sin to solve His problems. How many people do you know that when the going gets rough, the first thing they do is head for the bar? That is a sign of a lack of character and a lack of backbone in that person, because they will find no answers in the bar. It only multiplies the problems and makes them worse. Rather than just the problem they had, now they have two - the one they had and now the hang-over.

Jesus never resorted to any such thing. We have a high priest who knows by experience what's going on with us. Yet no matter how the heat was on and how tightly somebody turned the screws down on Him, He never resorted to sin to bale Himself out. And we don't have to either. Jesus went to God. We have a high priest who understands and knows and cares, unlike the view of Thomas Jefferson. Jesus cares. Cast all your care on Him, because He cares. That's the kind of high priest that we have.

> Heb 4:16
> 16 Let us therefore come boldly unto the throne of grace, that we may obtain mercy, and find grace to help in time of need.

Let us come boldly to the throne of grace. I like people who are bold. I am not very comfortable around a person who is real timid. I like boldness. I like people who know who they are, what they have, and what they believe. This verse says that we are to come exactly like that to the throne of grace.

I've seen so many Christians who were so timid and had a false sense of humility. God only knows what it was based on, but it was not Scripture. They act like they're ashamed to go before God, and if they did go before Him in prayer, all they did was beg, weep, and whine and cry. This is not what the Bible says to do. When we understand the priestly ministry of Jesus Christ, we won't be wimps as we approach God. Let us come BOLDLY to the throne of grace, not backing up as though we're not sure if the door to the throne is going to be locked. No, the door is wide open to us. But when we go in whimpering and stammering, we are acting in unbelief. We're saying that we don't believe in His high priestly ministry. We're saying, "I don't believe that the priesthood of Christ is going to work for me. I'm going to try to sneak around, do an end run, and slip in from another direction." But the Bible says to come boldly to the throne of grace.

How To Exercise God's Megaton Power Now

I talk to God just like He's a person, because He is. I use language just like I'm using with you. God understands the way I speak, He made me the way I am. I'm not irreverent, but I get to the point. If I've got something to say to Him, I say it, and I'll do it boldly because the Word says that I'm to do it boldly.

Stop being a spiritual wimp! The Bible says that we have a high priest who is always on the job, and based on His high priestly ministry we have a right to come to God boldly. Go boldly and say, "This is what I need! I'm asking You to meet it, in the Name of Jesus." If you can base a need on Scripture, you have every right to go to God boldly. You also have every right to boldly expect that need to be met. Because when you go to the throne of grace based upon Scripture, and you lay that Scripture out before the Son of God as your high priest, He picks up the fact that you're saying the same thing with your lips that God said when He had His Word written down, and He in turn says the same identical thing to God Almighty. Is it any wonder that we're told to come boldly!

When we go to the throne of God afraid of what's going to happen, it's the same as saying, "I don't believe the Word. I don't believe the priesthood ministry of Jesus. I don't believe God. I don't believe anything." Why are we to come boldly? So that we might obtain mercy and find grace to help in time of need. Look back at the verse. Does it say that you might get a little grace and mercy? Does it say that if the sun is shining you might get a little grace and mercy? Does it say that if God is having a good day you might get a little grace and mercy? Does it say that if your favorite football team wins the championship you might get a little grace and mercy? NO, it says, "Come boldly to the throne of grace, that we may obtain ...."

A lot of people don't obtain because they don't believe that they're going to obtain; therefore, they are not bold in their approach to God. God doesn't like it when we act like a wimp in His presence. He wants us to come to Him boldly, because we have every right to come to Him with both barrels blazing. We have every right to come to Him like a steam engine. We have every right to come to Him like an atom bomb. Come boldly! God likes that! Otherwise, He would not have said it. People, I didn't write this Scripture, I'm just teaching it.

How To Exercise God's Megaton Power Now

People don't obtain because they are timid. They're timid because they just don't believe. When you don't believe, you're not going to get. But when you get bold, that means you believe. And when you believe, brother and sister, you're going to receive.

Take advantage of the fact that you have a high priest. When you say the same thing in your prayers that the Word of God says - that's your confession - the high priest will intercept what you say, relay it to God, and the wheels will be set in motion for a miracle to happen in your life. Therefore, come boldly that you may obtain! Listen, if that Scripture said for us to go to the throne of grace like a whimpering scaredy cat that we may obtain, then I'd do that way. But it doesn't say that. It says to come boldly based on the priestly ministry of Jesus and the fact that He can identify with everything in our lives.

Come boldly, come boldly, come boldly. Get to the point with God; get in there and just say it - that you may obtain. You're going in there to obtain something. Listen, when I go, I'm not leaving empty handed. There are things that I need, and I'm going to get or obtain them. God is a God who is on the other end of the word OBTAIN. He's dispensing, we're receiving. He's giving, we've getting. Go in there and stay there until you obtain.

Do you have a need in you life? Then go to the throne, base that need on the Word of God, and go in boldly. God is in the grace and mercy business. GO OBTAIN! I like the word obtain. There is something about it that rings good with me. Some words are solid words, and some words seem to be flimsy words. The word obtain has a hard-core, solid, foundational ring to it. I like to obtain.

God set this system up so that you can approach Him with your head up. And why shouldn't your head be up? You're a son of God, and the seed of Abraham, and that makes you somebody! Hallelujah! Go with your head up and boldly OBTAIN.

The Abrahamic Covenant guarantees healing, prosperity, well-being for your family members, in addition to your salvation. What is your need? If you can trace it down to one of these areas, you can get it, you can obtain it. It's been promised to you. Quit being a wimp, state your case, lay it out, claim the promise, confess the Scripture, and expect to obtain, because you are going to find grace and mercy to help in your time of need.

How You Can Exercise God's *Megaton Power* Now

CHAPTER 11

STEP BY STEP GUIDE TO EXPLOSIVE, POWERHOUSE RESULTS WHEN YOU PRAY FOR THE HEALING, PROSPERITY AND WELL-BEING GOD PROMISED YOU AND YOUR FAMILY IN THE ABRAHAMIC COVENANT

The subject of this last chapter is how to pray for things with power. There is a way in which we must deal with certain situations in life. If we deal with them God's way, then we can get on top of the problem quickly. But if we try to take short cuts, we won't get the results that we would like to see.

I want to direct the teaching in this chapter specifically to prayer for the sick. There are provisions for healing contained in the Abrahamic Covenant. So when I preach on the Abrahamic Covenant, I aim it toward the sick. When I finish a message many people respond and are healed, because God taught me how to deal with sickness.

How To Exercise God's Megaton Power Now

Many people have written me for a copy of the prayer I've prayed on TBN when I've prayed for the sick. I don't have a copy of that prayer. However, this chapter explains what I do when I minister to the sick and also how I do it.

The first thing I do in ministering to the sick is Praise the Lord. The Bible says that God inhabits the praises of His people. So I praise the Lord to bring Him on the scene. If He inhabits the praises of His people, then I'll bring Him in with praise. So I say to the Lord several times "Bless you Lord. Bless you Lord. Bless you Lord." Then when I feel in my spirit that he is there with me, I go on to actually pray for the sick person I'm ministering to.

Look at John 16:23-24

> 23 And in that day ye shall ask me nothing. Verily, verily, I say unto you, Whatsoever ye shall ask the Father in my name, he will give it you.
> 24 Hitherto have ye asked nothing in my name: ask, and ye shall receive, that your joy may be full.

When somebody comes to me to be ministered to in the area of healing, the second thing I do is go to God in prayer. I ask God for two things. Number one, I ask God to remove all the pain and discomfort from that person's body. I ask Him to do that even before I ask Him to heal the person, because sometimes they are hurting, and they need for the pain to leave. I will address the pain, and then ask the Father in the Name of Jesus, "Father, in Jesus' Name, I ask that You remove all the pain and discomfort in this person's body now." Then the second thing I pray for is that God will heal the person with a complete healing.

I was in a meeting once and had a most unusual circumstance happen. I had a young lady with a curved spine come forward for prayer. Her spine was in the shape of an "S". I began to pray first of all that God would remove the pain that was in her body, because she was experiencing severe pain, and it immediately left her body. Then I asked Him to straighten and heal her back. Well, with the pain gone, I assumed that she was completely healed. However, at least for the time I was there, the curve in her backbone did not disappear. This told me that in time, if she would continue to do what I taught that church to do (and what I'm going to teach you to do in this chapter), her backbone would straighten out. This was a new experience for me though, because I had never seen someone who was in that much pain be delivered from the pain without the healing being totally manifested. So, the second thing that I do when I'm ministering healing to someone is pray, "Father, take away the pain and heal this person's body."

The next thing that I do is turn my attention to the Devil. Once I pray to the Father, then I have some things to say to the Devil. So, I pray to God, then speak directly to the Devil.
Let's look at Matthew 12:28-29.

> 28   But if I cast out devils by the Spirit of God, then the kingdom of God is come unto you.
> 29   Or else how can one enter into a strong man's house, and spoil his goods, except he first bind the strong man? and then he will spoil his house.

In ministering healing to the sick, I have learned that the Devil is the strong man. I have known this theologically for years, but it's only been in the last year that I have actually begun to apply it in my own healing ministry. I didn't think it was necessary. But since I have learned to apply this truth in praying for the sick, the results in healings has actually doubled, which means that you cannot leave something out. It may seem unimportant to you, but if it's in the Scripture, it's important.

But, I left this particular concept out when praying. What exactly are you talking about, Brother Jay? Simply this - you bind the Devil in that person's body, specifically in the area of their sickness. I talk to the Devil and say, "Satan, I bind you in this person's body in the Name of Jesus. Specifically in the area of this sickness, I bind you. I render you powerless. There is nothing more that you can do to this person. You are bound in Jesus' Name."

Now having done that, what does that enable me to do? It enables me to enter his house and spoil his goods. His "house" is the person who is being messed with in the area of their health. His "goods" happens to be the disease that he has caused in their body. The "housekeepers" over his house are demons. So after I pray to God, I immediately bind the Devil.

I was preaching a meeting for a Baptist pastor outside of Tulsa, Oklahoma a few weeks ago. The largest part of the membership of this church was Spirit-filled and believed in healing. This pastor had seen me on the Trinity Broadcasting Network. He called and wanted me to come minister to his church. The second night I was there, I looked out at the congregation and saw a tall, handsome young man watching me with great interest as I ministered healing during the alter call. Early the next morning he called me and asked if he could spend an hour with me. I said, "Yes." He met me in the pastor's office about 10:00 A.M. This man told me that he was from Australia. He said that he had heard of people being healed but had never been in a meeting where he could watch it happen.

He came back to the service that night, and I noticed that when I gave the alter call, this man came down and stood right behind the person I was praying for. He was looking over their shoulder at me, watching everything I did with my hands and listening to everything that I said. He had a yellow legal pad and a pocket full of pencils, and he was taking notes as fast as he could write. When I finished praying for that person and went to the next, he went go with me. He did this every night of the meeting.

The last night he came to me and said, "Brother Jay, 99% of the people that you have prayed for this week have been healed. There have been 50 people healed, I counted them."

How did this happen? Because I learned that I cannot short-change the method that God has given for dealing with the sick, or any problem for that matter. I was trying to enter the strong man's house and spoil his goods when he was still in control of it. And Jesus said, "How can you do that until you bind the strong man?"

So, I learned it the hard way. I finally started binding him, and God began to do things through me that He could not do before, because I was leaving out the third major step after asking God to heal. Once the strong man is bound, then I am absolutely free to pillage is house and his goods any way I want to. Verse 29 says that when the strong man is bound, then he will spoil his house. Do you see that? Then he will, he will. I began to think about that and said to myself, "O.K. I'm going to bind that sucker, and then I WILL spoil his goods." So I did. I bound him and then said to him, "Now I'm fixing to spoil your playhouse, buddy!"

When I got saved God placed inside me an absolute reverence for Scripture. Once I'm convinced that I know and understand what it says, I'll walk out on it; I'll stand on it. I have never had God let me down, and I have trusted and proved His Word many times in my life. My life depends on God's Word. The promises of God have sustained me for many years, absolutely sustained me. Someone once told me that he felt I was a little slow in grasping certain things about God's Word. Maybe I am, but you can bet that when I DO get it, I'll know absolutely without doubt what God said, and I'll know how it applies to me. Once I KNOW what God Almighty has said about something, I won't go off half-cocked, but I WILL walk it out. I'll risk myself to stand on it. I've never had it blow up in my face.

After I bind the strong man, then I begin to deal with the things in his house. The first thing I deal with are his housekeepers. Who are the housekeepers? They're demons. However, you won't get very far with the demons until you bind the strong man; because the demons don't have any authority, but the Devil does. The demons get what authority and power they do have from the Devil. So, let's deal with the demons. Turn to Mark 16:17.

> 17 And these signs shall follow them that believe;
> In my name shall they cast out devils; they shall
> speak with new tongues;

If Jesus says that I can cast out devils or demons in His Name, and demons are the housekeepers in Satan's house, then what am I going to do next? Well, many illnesses are caused by demonic activity. You would probably be surprised how many illnesses are caused by plain, old demons. So, I have to deal with that sickness based on my rights in Mark 16. I'll clean the house by calling out or casting out the demons. I say, "You foul spirit of infirmity, I command you in the Name of Jesus to come out. Take your pain and disease, damage and discomfort, go to the pit and stay there." I'll labor on this point until I know the demon has heard me, because when I have his attention he must do what I tell him to do in Jesus' Name. So I say, "I cast you out, in the Name of Jesus. Come out right now."

Then I will say to them, "Do not relocate and hide elsewhere in this person's body." They will try and do that. I've seen the place where the demon is located in the body turn red. It might not have been red when they came for prayer, but it'll turn red, as if I've embarrassed the demon. The red spot will sometimes move around to another place. The pain, rather than immediately coming out, will move to another part of the body. That's why I tell it not to relocate and hide. I've see it work, and the red spot leave the body.

The next thing I do is deal with the sickness itself. The Scriptural justification to do this is found in John's Gospel.

> John 14:13-14
> 13   And whatsoever ye shall ask in my name, that will I do, that the Father may be glorified in the Son.
> 14   If ye shall ask any thing in my name, I will do it.

Look at the word ask in verse 14. This is the Greek word AITEO. I talked about this in a previous chapter, but let's look at it again - it's important. That word, when it relates to a thing, should be translated "command". When it relates to God, it should be translated "strongly ask".

Look at the word **whatsoever** in verse 13 and the word **thing** in verse 14. In the Greek language these words are direct objects of the word **ask**. The word **ask** can be used in relationship to God, but we do not command God. The Greeks had more than one word for **ask**. There is the regular word for **ask**, then there is the one which means **ask as strongly as you can**. But when it relates to an "object" or an "it", the word should be translated **command**, because you cannot **ask** an "it".

Here we are told to ask for a **whatsoever** in one verse and a **thing** in the next verse. Therefore, the word **ask** should be translated

How To Exercise God's Megaton Power Now

command. Notice what Jesus says in verse 13, "**Whatsoever** you shall **command** in my Name, that will I do." Then in verse 14, "If you shall **command** any **thing** in my Name, I will do it."

So my next move, based on the Scripture, is to attack the sickness by telling it what to do in Jesus' Name. Is sickness a "thing"? Is it a "whatsoever"? Is it an it, a "thing"? Sure it is. So I attack it in the Name of Jesus, commanding it to do something. What do I tell it to do? I command it to die. Die at the roots, dry up, release the person, and come out.

Several years ago, there was a young lady in the hospital in Galveston, Texas who was diagnosed with terminal cancer. I drove to the hospital several times a week and taught her the principles of healing which are contained in the Abrahamic Covenant. She did not have a Charismatic, full-gospel background. She was raised in the Baptist church. So, she had to be taught that healing actually belonged to her. Over a period of about six weeks, in the coldest part of the year, three times a week I drove all the way to Galveston and taught this daughter of Abraham about Abraham's blessings. When her eyes were opened to see that healing really was taught in the Bible, then I laid hands on her body, prayed for her, and that cancer died. There was a growth on her back that was killing her. It dissolved and left her body. She is still healed today, praise God. There are only a few people in the world who have survived when diagnosed with this type of cancer.

This lady was healed by the power of God because I commanded the cancer to die at the roots, dry up, and come out of her body. Jesus said, "Whatsoever you ask in my Name, that's what I'm going to do," provided what I command is based on Scripture. Can I base a command for disease to die on Scripture? You better believe I can. Because the Abrahamic Covenant guaranteed healing to the Abrahamic Seed Group, and I am a part of that group. Therefore, I am authorized to give any form of a command that I can base on Scripture. I can give you Scripture to prove that healing belongs to Christians until you turn blue in the face.

Someone told me the other day that they saw a preacher on television who said that all the Spiritual gifts had passed away, they are not used any more. If I could meet this brother, I would jangle his theology so bad that he wouldn't be able to find his way home.

The Spiritual gifts are operating now. Every time I finish a healing meeting, and I know that I've been instrumental in seeing even one person healed, I am absolutely awed by it. To know that God used ME, He let ME be a channel through which He flowed to touch somebody boggles my mind. I am humbled by such a thing. So, I tell that sickness what to do. I'll make a command on it. "I command you in the Name of Jesus to die." I speak the death sentence right into it.

After I command the sickness to die, then I speak to the pain. I tell the pain what to do. Is pain a "whatsoever"? Is it an "anything"? Yes, it is. Looking back over the years of ministry and the meetings that God has let me do across the country, I would say that God has led me into a ministry against pain. It amazes me. But I've seen many people relieved of pain as I prayed for them.

There was a woman in a meeting of mine who had lived with pain for years. As I laid my hands on that dear lady and prayed, I saw the relief come - I saw it in her face. She still had a small amount of pain though, so I laid hands on her again and prayed again. I saw more relief come into her face. The third time I prayed the pain completely left her. She jumped up and down and began shouting, because she had not been without pain for a long time. This woman's doctor was a member of the church and was in this service. He stood and watched God do in a matter of a few minutes what he had not been able to do over many, many years of medical treatment.

Attack pain in the Name of Jesus. Tell it, "Pain, come out of this body in the Name of Jesus. Go to the pit and stay there. Discomfort, in the Name of Jesus, I command that you leave, go to the pit and stay there." Pain will leave. Why does this happen? Because it is a "whatsoever", and I've been told by Jesus that I can say whatever I want to a "whatsoever" and it will do what I say.

As a denominational preacher my biggest hurdle was getting enough guts to even try this. I asked God, "What if I do this and nothing happens?" He told me to try it anyway. I said, "I'm scared." He replied, "You've never been scared of anything. Get on with the program." So I did. Sure enough, it worked. The more it worked, the bolder I got. Listen, you can get bold enough to attack hell with a squirt gun if God tells you to.

If what I am after is a "thing" or a "whatsoever", I'll go at it. James wrote that faith without works is dead. You must act on the Word. Jesus told us to command a thing or a whatsoever, and He would do it.

The next thing I do in praying for the sick is to speak healing.

> Mark 16:18
> 18 They shall take up serpents; and if they drink any deadly thing, it shall not hurt them; they shall lay hands on the sick, and they shall recover.

I actually speak healing into a person's body. I say, "In the Name of Jesus, I command that you be healed." I lay hands on them and expect them to recover. I've seen them heal immediately as I watched; I've seen them heal through a process of time, but the point is that they got healed.

"They shall lay hands on the sick, and they shall recover." So, I lay hands on them and touch them. Let me give you a word of caution about this. Men, be very careful where you put your hands when praying for a lady. Nobody can ever say that I ever touched a lady improperly when I prayed for her. If a woman has an illness where your hands, as a man, should not go, you call for a Godly woman to come pray with you, and let her lay her hands on the woman. Be **very, very** careful.

Let me address something else at this point. There is no one that I have ever prayed for who can say that I shoved them to the floor to make it appear that they were slain in the Spirit when they weren't. People who do this are trying to convince others that God is producing results through them that He's not doing. They're trying to impress people. They may get people lined up on the floor, but very rarely do they get anyone healed. I do not like phony people! Frankly, I don't care what people think about me. I care what God thinks about me, and beyond that, I just don't care. I'm a man unto God, not unto men.

How To Exercise God's Megaton Power Now

Let's go back to healing people, praise God. So, I command the person to be healed. "I speak healing into you, in the Name of Jesus. I COMMAND that you be healed."

Let me share some more practical things with you. There is a belief in Pentecostal and Charismatic churches that if a person is prayed for one time and doesn't get healed, then that person must not have any faith. That is baloney!

When I pray for a person, I will ask that person, "How do you feel? Is there any difference in how you feel now than before I prayed?" Sometimes they will answer, "Well, I'm receiving my healing." Well, that is not what I asked. I asked, "How do you feel?" I don't know unless you tell me.

Sometimes they will tell me that they feel a little better. So I'll ask, "On a scale of one to ten, how much change is there in the way you feel." If they tell me maybe about a five, then I know I've got the job half done. What do I do then? First of all, I'm not embarrassed to pray again. Suppose I pray again, and there is no change. I'm still not embarrassed. It's not my Word. God is the one who said for me to lay hands on the sick and they would recover. I'm just doing what He told me to do. He's the one who has the problem, not me. So, I'll pray for the person again, doing what I feel like the Spirit of God is leading me to do. If I need to go through the entire process again - pray to God, ask Him to take away the pain, ask Him to heal the body, bind the Devil, cast out the demons, kill the disease - if I have to go through every step again, I'll do it. Usually the second time I will not have to go through every step, but if I feel led of God to repeat every word, I'll repeat every word. I'll deal with it, until I've done the job.

Remember, I'm not embarrassed. This is what I'll do. I pray again, "In the Name of Jesus Christ, disease, I command that you die at the roots. Dry up and come out. Pain and discomfort, I command that you leave. And now, I command you to heal. In the Name of Jesus, heal." I'll stop and ask, "How do you feel?" By this time, everyone is getting involved, because they see that I'm involved in a battle. I'll stay with it until it breaks, or I begin to see, by what they tell me, that the healing has begun and is on the way. Then I'll back off and say to them, "You keep doing what you saw me do, and this sickness will completely leave your body."

How To Exercise God's Megaton Power Now

There are a lot of silly, religious cliches around as to why someone may not receive immediate healing. I've already mentioned the one about the person having no faith for healing. However, the problem could be the one doing the praying - he just wasn't consistent. I would like to be able to say that I pray one time, and everyone is healed immediately. But you need to read the parable of the importunate (this is another word for persistent) widow in Luke 18. Find out how she received. Brother, she stayed with it until she got what she was after, and Jesus tells us to do the very same thing.

So, I'm not one bit embarrassed about praying more than one time for someone. I have absolutely no patience with preachers who will pray one time, and if the person is not healed right then and there, make them feel like a dog because they were not healed.

The point I'm making is, if you can't tell by now, don't quit, stay with it! I'll stay with it until the healing has begun, and then instruct them to continue to do what I've been doing, and usually within a matter of days the sickness is gone. I am firmly convinced that if a person will consistently apply the Name of Jesus Christ, that there is no any disease in the world that can stand up again it. There are many powerful diseases - cancer, AIDS, heart attacks - those are awesome sounding names of diseases. But there is a NAME that is above every other name, including cancer or any other name - THE NAME OF JESUS! I am convinced of this one thing - if you will consistently go against any thing using the Name of Jesus, you can melt the hinges off it's door.

When Jesus said to make the command in His Name against a "whatsoever" or a "thing", then I have to ask myself, "Is this a whatsoever, is this a thing?" If it is, it's name is Mud, because I'm going after it.

There is a warfare anointing that comes on me when it's time to minister to the sick. When it comes, awesome things happen. I've had people wait until a service was over and the anointing gone, then come to me and ask me to do for them what I was doing in the healing line. They waited when they should have come when I asked. I can still operate in faith for them, but when faith is combined with that anointing, then powerful things happen. So when the anointing is present to heal, that's when you move out to receive. That's when real miracles begin to happen.

This is how to deal with the sick. This is the way to get results. It has been tested not only by me, but by others also. It works, my brother and sister. Take the Name of Jesus - cast out devils, lay hands on the sick, and stand back and watch them recover!

You have the power now! Use it!

People Across The Country Are Saying:

The Most Life Changing Thing Ever Written On Healing And Prosperity Are The Author's Four Books On The Abrahamic Covenant:

- **What Are Abraham's Blessings Anyway?**

This Volume Explains Why Jesus. *MUST H*eal and Prosper You Now.

- **What've They Done With Abraham's Blessings?**

This Volume Destroys The Modernistic Denial That Healing and Prosperity Belong To Christians Now

- **The Unbroken Force of Abraham's Blessings**

The Main Reason To Deny That Healing and Prosperity Belong To Christians Now, Defined, Examined, Refuted and Destroyed

- **How To Obtain Abraham's Blessings**

A Simple, Step by Step Guide To Obtaining The Healing, Prosperity and Well-being For Every Member of Your Family That God Promised You in The Abrahamic Covenant.

These Four Books Will Build Your Faith To A Fever Pitch. Order Yours Now, Here, Today. You'll Be Glad You Did!